MAHARANI

Memoirs of a Rebellious Princess

Brinda, Maharani of Kapurthala

by
Elaine Williams

Illustrated with Photographs

Rupa & Co

Copyright © Elaine Williams 1954, 2000

Originally published by Henry Holt

First in Rupa Paperback 2003

Published by

Rupa & Co

7/16, Ansari Road, Daryaganj,
New Delhi 110 002

Sales Centres:

Allahabad Bangalore Chandigarh Chennai
Dehradun Hyderabad Jaipur Kathmandu
Kolkata Ludhiana Mumbai Pune

All rights reserved.
No part of this book may be reproduced, or transmitted in any form or by any means, graphic, electronic, or mechanical, including photocopying, recording, taping or by any information storage or retrieval system, without the permission in writing from the publisher.

ISBN 0-595-09428-7

Cover design by Grade Design

This edition is for sale in Indian Subcontinent only

Printed in India by
Rekha Printers Pvt. Ltd,
A-102/1 Okhla Industrial Area, Phase-II,
New Delhi-110 020

Maharani

PREFACE

My first meeting with Princess Brinda, Maharani of Kapurthala, took place at tea in the crystal-chandeliered dining room of the old and elegant Hotel Sulgrave on Park Avenue. The appointment was arranged by my literary agent after I agreed to consider authoring a book on the maharani's extraordinary royal life. She was anxious for her story to be told and although I was a very young woman at the time I was touched by the elderly monarch's poignant story of a princess manipulated and betrayed.

Despite my deep sympathy for her plight it was crucial that as author I retain the freedom of my own perceptions. So, before work could begin it was necessary for the maharani to accept the stipulation not to interfere with my text or read the manuscript before publication. The maharani agreed and the project went forward with a series of meetings and interviews.

Hers was a fascinating tale of contrasts and conflicts set against the colorful background of India at the height of royal excess as it emerged from the 19th century, and in Paris where an aristocratic mecca welcomed displaced royalty into the jazz age.

She was a ravishing beauty then, who with her princely husband, destined to be maharaja, was the toast of Paris in the 1920s and 30s. They were the *"jewels in the crown"* of French society, mingling with deposed European crowned heads including King Alfonso of Spain and Queen Marie of Rumania, along with famed artists and writers of jazz-age Paris. Cole Porter wrote the tune *"Let's Misbehave"* for Princess Brinda, Gaylord

Hauser (health food mentor to Greta Garbo) praised her beauty and creaminess of skin which he claimed was due to her vegetarian diet while famed British photographer Cccii Beaton captured her in an exquisite portrait.

On her 1936 visit to New York she dazzled *Vanity Fair* magazine who wrote. *"Princess Brinda of Kapurthala, daughter-in-law of the Maharaja, had every woman green with envy. Her collection of jewels would make Tiffany and Cartier turn in their vaults. Emeralds the size of walnuts hung from her ears and diamond necklaces by the yard circled her throat."*

But all that ended when the old maharaja insisted his son take another wife to produce a male heir for the royal dynasty. Princess Brinda had three daughters but could bear no more children. A second wife was not uncommon in India but years spent in Europe had westernized the princess and the idea of supplanting her in this way was humiliating and unacceptable.

The maharani began to live a life separate from the prince and became something of a wanderer. The cachet of her royal status made her welcome to socialite friends all over the world but her grief was still there and she was experiencing financial difficulties. One day, she opened a box to show me six or seven huge emeralds resting on black velvet. They were incredible, flawless, the luminous green of the Aegean Sea. She was loath to part with her precious emeralds but the renowned jewelers, Van Cleef & Arpels, had offered a munificent sum to acquire them.

After the book was published we lost touch for some time. When I heard from the maharani again I was married and living in Goshen, New York with my husband and three young children on a neglected estate in a old rambling house which we were restoring. She hoped to stay with us for a week and I looked forward to seeing her again.

She made herself at home, even rolled up her sleeves and went into the kitchen to teach me how to cook a real Indian curry, not the cream sauce with curry powder I had known before. This was a marvel of onions, spices, vegetables or meat, longcooked and succulent.

The maharani was appalled at my involvement with my children and the household. "Elaine, you have too much talent to waste your time on all this nonsense!" she told me.

On the other hand, she was still the princess. Our Dutch housekeeper came in early to take care of the children and do the cooking and I was able to sleep a bit longer in the morning. However, the maharani couldn't let me rest. She'd come to my door at eight o'clock and bang on it shouting, "Elaine, Elaine, I must have my tea!" Grudgingly, I'd tear myself out of bed and go down to prepare her breakfast. But I also understood her need.

The maharani cut quite a dashing figure the afternoon we took her to the Hambletonian Races, Goshen's claim to fame. She wore a Parisian outfit of a gleaming white satin tunic with flowing pants and ropes of pearls hanging over her neck. She showed me the ring on her finger, a large emerald set in gold. It looked flawless to me but she explained it was a faux stone, made in Paris. "People think it's real," she whispered, with a laugh. "They can't believe a maharani would wear a fake."

Before leaving she invited me to India. "Come stay with me at my palace in Kapurthala and write."

It was a tempting offer but I couldn't leave my young family nor did I feel it safe to bring them along to India. Some time later I made my first visit to India but sadly Princess Brinda was no longer alive.

The maharani was a bit of a character, strongminded and imperious, a mix of spirituality and royal entitlement but I'd grown fond of her. She had been a unique experience in my life, a peek into the astonishing world of imperial India that had vanished forever.

Elaine Williams

Chapter One

As I waited with my governess in the cool palace gardens of Kapurthala I shivered with anticipation. Engaged to the son of the Maharaja of Kapurthala for three years, now finally I was to meet him. Our marriage had been arranged by our parents three years ago when I was seven and my husband-to-be nine, but the Tika Raja and I had been kept apart. Now I was nearly ten and it was time to be growing up.

At the time of our betrothal, perhaps I had some curiosity about my marriage—which was being arranged with such excitement—but not much. As a small Hindu princess I was not expected to evince any interest in my future life; it was only necessary for me to obey my parents and mind my manners. I knew that someday I had to get married; I also understood that the choice was not up to me. The choice, in fact, had been made by the Maharaja of Kapurthala. He knew that my family was of the highest

2

caste and that my father, befallen by the calamity—in India—of having four daughters, would welcome a match to the heir of the wealthy state of Kapurthala. And as my mother told me later on, I apparently was as a child just as pretty as the blood of my ancestors was pure. So, while the engagement festivities raged about the palace, I played happily with my sisters, never believing that one day life would change so much for me.

We were formally introduced three years after our engagement, by Western standards a belated introduction, but in the East since orthodox Hinduism forbids a husband to look upon his wife's face before the wedding day it was, if anything, premature. Our meeting was carefully chaperoned by my governess, the Tika Raja's mother who was senior Maharani, and his two brothers.

Waiting beneath the damp trees in the palace garden for the Tika Raja to appear, I was suddenly apprehensive. All my curiosity had fled and I wanted only to be back home again with my face buried in the knees of my ayah who knew only too well that I was still a little girl. But even at ten I knew there was no turning back. I had been taught submission well and there never was any question but that I must do my duty.

So I went forward, my mouth trembling with shyness, my heart pounding against my new dress, to meet my future husband. He stood there looking at me without saying a word. What a strange boy he is, I thought in disappointment, for he seemed quite different from the boys who romped with me inside our palace walls, screaming down the winding corridors with much teasing and laughter.

3

Even at twelve the Tika Raja was old and serious with dark, brooding eyes and a tense, unhappy face. He said nothing but stared at me without changing his expression. I stood in silence, trying to realize that this stranger had something to do with me and in that moment lost my childhood forever. For the second time that afternoon fear swept over me as I gazed at the boy into whose hands my life had been given.

Amarjat Singh, his stepbrother, broke the silence. "Let's play," he suggested. With relief we followed his suggestion. It was lovely to be a child again and romp about the lawns with the three princes, but whenever I looked back at that afternoon I remembered it not as a child but as a woman.

Our forthcoming marriage had been arranged when the Pandit Mirtunja, a spiritual leader in the court of my father's friend, the Maharaja of Kapurthala, visited us to ask for my small hand in marriage to the Maharaja's eldest son and heir, Paramjit Singh Tika Raja. In many ways it was a good match. Kapurthala, one of the first Sikh states, was both larger and wealthier than our state of Jubbal, and for many years the Maharaja and my father had been close friends.

But to my mother a marriage between her small princess and the house of Kapurthala was a shocking disgrace. As the daughter of one of the most ancient of Hindu dynasties, Rajput, she believed it humiliating to consider an alliance with the Kapurthalas. They, too, had been Rajput centuries before, but had since embraced the Sikh faith. To my mother they were now outcasts.

Sikhism, a Hindu reform movement started in the fifteenth century by Guru Nanak, represented to my mother the antithesis of everything she believed in. Not only did they ask equality for women, both religious and legal, but they denied reincarnation, a basic tenet of orthodox Hinduism, and—worst of all—refused to accept caste. In the Sikh faith a man of any religion or caste, even an untouchable, was accepted as an equal. For a woman of royal birth, uneducated except for religious instruction, indoctrinated since birth in Hindu orthodoxy, a merger with a family of the radical Sikh faith was unthinkable.

Shortly after our visitor from Kapurthala arrived, I noticed that a profound change had come over my mother. Until that time her face had held only serenity and warmth and a gentle smile for me when I had run to her from play for comfort. Much of her time was spent in prayer and meditation and often I loved to steal into her room and sit in the corner to feel her quietness about me.

But suddenly all this changed. Now I found her rocking silently in her room with tears streaming down her face. She seemed distraught and unhappy and her eyes were red and sad from weeping. Even I, happy and thoughtless child that I was, became disturbed and frightened by her change. Finally, I could bear it no longer and weeping too, flung myself down at her side and begged to know what terrible fate had befallen us.

Fighting back the tears, she told me that my marriage to the heir of Kapurthala had been arranged against her wishes. Instantly I was relieved. It had always been clear to me that someday I would have to be married and since I knew I had no choice in the decision it mattered little which one of the eligible princes my parents chose for me.

5

The day of marriage was always many years away from the childhood engagement, so to me the fuss seemed premature. I was interested in today, not tomorrow.

But I was touched by my mother's unhappiness and like all children had a quick and easy solution. "If you don't like it," I said, "then you must tell Father and make him stop this thing."

Mother shook her head sadly. "He has given his word of honor," she said. "Now it must be."

For a moment I tried to think about marriage, but it was too difficult. At seven marriage did not concern me and, with that thought, I hurried back to play.

It was not difficult for me, then, to shut my mind to unpleasantness. Up to that point my childhood had been surrounded by protection and happiness and I had no reason to believe this would ever change.

My life as a princess began in the palace of the hill state of Jubbal one January morning as the snow tumbled about the Himalayan mountains. My mother, who had married at eleven and borne two children before me—both of whom died in infancy—was just fourteen years old.

My father, Prince Gambhir Chand, was the younger brother of Jubbal's ruler, Rana Padam Chand. Our family had ruled the state of Jubbal for over thirty generations and tradition had it that originally our ancestors had descended from the Moon. The truth was, as I learned some years later, our family was but one of thirty-six Rajput clans who claimed descent from the Sun, Moon, or Sacred Fire; actually my ancestors came from Central Asia in the fifth century and married into Hindu families. Later they persuaded the Brahmins, the highest Hindu caste, to admit them into their caste and provide them with their fantastic ancestry. Our kingdom of Jubbal, about fifty miles east of Simla in northern India, had been founded about the year 1066 after the invasion by the Moslems.

Before the Moslems came, the Rajput women had been relatively free; they chose their own husbands, accompanied them in hunting and war, and, at their death, mounted the funeral pyre at their side. But, in order to escape defilement by the Moslems, severe restrictions were placed upon them. So purdah, or isolation with other women, and the heavy veiling came into effect. Originally meant as a protection, through the years it has been one of the most difficult burdens Indian women have had to bear.

It was in order to escape annihilation that our family fled from the plains to the foothills of the Himalayas and founded our little Rajput kingdom of Jubbal. It was there, in a rickety wooden palace made up of rambling rooms tacked to each other on the edge of a steep cliff, that I was born.

Immediately after my birth I was given away. Wrapped in a coarse blanket, I was handed to a low-born peasant woman who stood waiting outside the door to receive me. But my departure from the royal family was only temporary. It was a measure to placate the angry gods who had taken away my parents' first children; a few moments later the family priest bought me back for five silver rupees, or about $1.25, and I was returned to my mother's eager arms.

Even at birth we were surrounded by the ancient superstitions of Hinduism. Both mother and child were considered unclean and kept in almost total darkness for thirteen days. On the thirteenth day we were purified together with water from the sacred Ganges River and my father looked upon us for the first time.

As a young child my life was carefree and happy. I was high-spirited, restless, and often mischievous. Left largely in the care of servants, like most children I tried to take advantage of them as much as possible. As the eldest child I was in a good position to do this, since they felt I was closest to my parents. The servants themselves were lazy and corrupt and usually tried to take the line of least resistance. As a result my feelings about right and wrong were often sadly mixed.

One day I ran to my nurse, or ayah as we called her, begging for a piece of material to make my doll a sari. She had none, she told me, but as I teased and plagued her she grew tired of the argument and suggested, "Go quickly to your mother's room and take a piece of veil from her basket." Satisfied at last, I played happily with my dolls for the rest of the afternoon.

Later my mother called me to her room. "My child," she asked, "did you cut my veil?" Half realizing all along that I had done something wrong, I burst into tears at her question. Stammering, I explained that my ayah had given me permission. "Then we must ask Ayah," replied my mother calmly. Ayah's face was a studied blank as she answered my mother respectfully. No, she didn't know what I was talking about; it was the first time she had heard that I needed cloth for my doll.

Naturally, I was punished for destructiveness and lying. But deeper than my childish dislike of punishment was my frustration and outrage at being misunderstood. The world of grownups, I decided, was a dangerous place. In the future I would try to be more wary.

The one thing I did not lack was companionship. The palace was fairly overrun with children of assorted ages, since we followed the Hindu custom of several families living together in the sprawling palace. And, of course, there was my father's other family.

My mother was his second wife and his first, or senior wife as she was called, lived in the palace as well, with her several children. I saw little of her—she occupied a completely separate apartment—but I regarded her children as my brothers and sisters and thought it not strange at all that my father had two wives.

We, too, had our own apartment and servants, and my father lived in a third apartment on another floor. Like many Hindu husbands he considered his time completely his own. Daily he visited each of his wives, played a bit with his children, and retired to his own apartment where his life was unquestioned by either of his wives. My mother never spoke of his first wife. In some way it was almost as though she did not exist for us.

Altogether there were about thirty children in the palace, so although we were not permitted beyond the courtyards we never felt that the world outside offered more for children than the fun and mischief that went on inside its walls.

One of our favorite games was doctor and patient, a pastime we thought we invented. But since then I have discovered that children all over the world play the same game and have been told that the meaning behind it is universal as well.

In our case, we were fascinated by vaccination. Not long after my uncle (ordinarily opposed to modern medicine) decided to vaccinate the entire palace, we decided to follow his example. Most of the windows in the palace were closed not with glass but by wooden shutters. The throne room, however, was an exception, so one day about a dozen of us broke a window in there and began vaccinating each other with splinters of glass. We bribed the little ones with apples to stifle their screams while the rest of us bravely allowed ourselves to be scratched until blood gushed. At least one of the children developed a mild case of blood poisoning from our game, and afterward the rest of us, nursing our wounds, were happy to leave glass windows alone.

My lessons were always a chore to me. I was easily bored by the endless droning of the teachers and anxious to escape as quickly as possible to the more exciting pastime of chasing my young companions up and down the twisting corridors. But again I had little choice in the matter. With the other children, I was taught to read and write Hindi by one of the *gurus* or religious teachers of my uncle's court. Our everyday language, Pahari, was a hill version of ancient Sanskrit and it was not until after my engagement that I learned to speak Hindustani, the language of most Indians.

Life in the palace followed its own routine. At seven I was awakened by my nurse, washed, and quickly dressed in tight-fitting silk trousers with a loose shirt of silk or muslin. On my head I wore the traditional *duputta,* or veil, but by midmorning it had usually slipped off onto my shoulders and was flying behind me as I raced about in play. Most of the time my feet were bare but on the coldest winter days I wore woolen socks under goatskin slippers.

Perhaps today it would be considered that we lived in a world of inconveniences but to us it seemed perfectly comfortable. Although the winters in northern India are bitterly cold, there was no central heating, only a charcoal brazier placed in the center of the room on a stone slab. Nor did we have running water or bathtubs. We were bathed in a small room by our nurse who stood us on a wooden plank and poured water over us. Our toilet was a hole in the floor of another room, connected to a straw-covered tray several floors below by a funnel. This tray was cleaned by sweepers of the untouchable or lowest caste who were forbidden to enter the palace.

It is difficult for a princess not to feel like a princess, especially in India where so much emphasis is placed upon caste and the importance of high birth. In many ways I must have been spoiled and the servants did their share to make me feel that I was someone special. It was only later in life as tragedy and disappointment came my way, as they do to everyone, that I began to feel less like a princess and more like any other human being.

Once when I was about five years of age, dressed in the costume of our province, I was attending a celebration. A ring of rubies and diamonds had been placed in my little pierced nose, in my ears which were pierced in six places were six jeweled earrings, and on my toe was a large ring.

My dress was bright red satin embroidered in green and gold and on my head bobbed a tiny golden veil. As I danced by a mirror I suddenly caught a glimpse of myself in it.

"Oh!" I exclaimed. "I'm such a pretty little girl!" and ran and kissed myself in the mirror.

All the guests laughed and petted me. How clever of the little princess to admire herself! So I was encouraged then and throughout my childhood to believe in my special importance; many times later in life I wished instead I had been taught more of the harsher facts of living.

In the morning after prayers came breakfast, a meal of hot milk, unleavened, whole-wheat bread fried in butter, and several sweets. We ate, squatting on stools two inches from the floor, from dishes of silver or brass. We did not use silverware but ate our food with our fingers, scooping it up with the help of the fried pancakes, a traditional part of the meal.

Religion plays an important part in the life of every Hindu family. We began each day by chanting long prayers from the epic poem, the Bhagavad-Gita (Song Celestial), which in poetic form is the essence of the Hindu religion. But to me the long verses meant nothing. I only knew that it was required for me to say them and I did, obediently and as quickly as possible. For one thing, we prayed in ancient Sanskrit. To an Indian child Sanskrit is about as meaningful as Latin is to a child of the West. Taught by rote, the meaning of our religion was not really explained; and perhaps even if I had understood it in my childish way, its deeper concept would still have been incomprehensible to me.

As a child, to me the world was everything; to a real

Hindu, the world is but another chance in his struggle to come closer to God. The Hindu religion differs from most religions in that, rather than encouraging man to work out his life on earth according to certain laws or even spiritual concepts, it urges him to accept his lot on earth uncomplainingly; in fact, it teaches him to disregard the world and concentrate on the life of the spirit and the world beyond. The man of God is explained by the Gita in this way:

> He knows bliss in the Atman *
> And wants nothing else.
> Cravings torment the heart;
> He renounces cravings.
> I call him illumined,
> Not shaken by adversity,
> Not hankering after happiness:
> Free from fear, free from anger,
> Free from the things of desire.
> I call him a seer and illumined.
>
> The bonds of his flesh are broken.
> He is lucky, and does not rejoice:
> He is unlucky, and does not weep.
> I call him illumined.
>
> The tortoise can draw in its legs:
> The seer can draw in his senses.
> I call him illumined.

Being born is considered a kind of punishment, for the spirit who reaches God is never born again. He has become so pure in heart that he finds eternal bliss. But others must

* Soul.

die, only to be born again in sorrow and suffering. Thus, in India the caste system has been acceptable for, according to the religion, the soul chooses its own parents as in each life it advances closer to God. A low birth is often considered an indication of the lack of progress made in the previous life, although this has little to do with achieving spiritual heights in a present life. From the lowest caste, or untouchables, have come many saints and teachers who achieved highest spirituality.

Hindus believe in one soul. This soul is without beginning and without end. It is indestructible and incorruptible, birthless and deathless. All human beings are part of this soul and the object of Hinduism is to merge each individual soul with this universal one. The realization of God is known as *yoga*, or the science of spirituality.

Through yoga there are four ways to reach God. *Karma-yoga* is the path of action. It teaches man to work but to work without thought of reward and to love his work more than he loves what that work accomplishes. Attachment is slavery, detachment is freedom, so man must view with indifference the rewards of success and the pain of failure. The goal of activity must be the increasing knowledge of the soul.

Bhakti-yoga is the path of worship. His religion is rich in ritual and ceremonies and begins and ends in love. For this love he seeks no return. He does not love God to achieve pleasure in life or happiness in heaven, but because God is love, beauty, and goodness. He asks nothing of God, only that He deal with him in His infinite wisdom. He does not fear God because in perfect love there can be no fear; through complete unselfishness his love is divine and the lover and the beloved become one.

Jnana-yoga is the philosophical path to God and the man who follows it uses the method of reasoning. He learns what is reality and meditates upon it. By means of his will power he renounces the unreal and through moral discipline and complete renunciation he tries to discover the immortal in himself and the universe.

Raja-yoga is the way for the mystic, through moral and ethical disciplines. With the help of posture and breathing the student of *raja-yoga* learns concentration and meditation in an attempt to learn the nature of the soul.

The goal of Hinduism is liberation from misery, from death, and from life. Man's true identity is God and only through ignorance has he limited himself to race, sex, caste, and creed. Life is the means by which he may rediscover his infinite soul but he can only go beyond death when he realizes his unity with the immortal.

For years I parroted the beautiful verses of the Gita, chanted the humble philosophy of the teachers, but in those days it held little meaning for me. As my life began to pass, however, the spirituality of my religion began to hold out more and more comfort to me and the fleeting pleasures of life seemed to dwindle in comparison with the infinite reward of God.

But that is a story of my later life, for my early years were certainly preoccupied with the world. In the beginning I was no child of heaven.

Chapter Two

For me the palace at Jubbal was a magic castle. There were over a hundred rooms in the sprawling wooden structure and endless twisting corridors, courtyards, and balconies where I played make-believe games with the thirty other children who lived in the palace.

Of all the children I was the most reckless. Proud of the fact that I could climb as well as any of the boys, I seized on every opportunity to prove it. One day when I was five I decided to climb out on the edge of a balcony on the third story. Teetering dangerously on the narrow wooden railing I held my breath in terror and took a step forward. Somehow I managed to maintain my balance. Then, full of confidence at my success, I turned my head to make sure my playmates were watching and shouted "Look at me!" As the last word left my lips my foot suddenly slipped and I fell three storys to the courtyard below.

16

It was a miracle that I wasn't killed. But I was far from unconscious. I lay on the ground screaming in pain and fright as servants rushed from everywhere to carry me back into the house. Blood was streaming from my face and when it was wiped away they saw that the whole side of my face was torn to the bone. My mother stood over me in horror, wringing her hands and crying that I would be disfigured for life. "What a fate for a girl," she moaned. "Now we will never be able to find her a husband."

Since my father had little faith in medicine, he would not call a doctor to treat me. No stitches were taken, no medication was applied. Instead, my father himself prepared a huge poultice of butter and sulphur. This was applied to my face and kept there with a cloth for over a month. When it was removed my cheek was completely smooth again except for an almost invisible scar. Modern science could not have done a better job.

But my uncle, Rana Padam Chand, the ruler of Jubbal, was not so lucky. His opposition to science ended in disaster, both for him and for our family.

My uncle, a high-strung man, had a nervous habit of plucking hairs from the back of his hand while engrossed in conversation. When I was about six an infection developed from this. Beginning as a simple infection, because of lack of treatment it gradually spread to his fingers, then up his arm. By this time it had developed into an acute case of blood poisoning and he was in an agony of suffering. It became necessary to amputate his hand and later his arm. But it was to no avail. He grew steadily worse and three months after the infection began it was clearly apparent that the Rana of Jubbal was a dying man.

As he lay on his deathbed he called my father to his side. "After my death," he whispered, "leave Jubbal. It is finished for you here now. Take your share of the fortune and go."

Shaken by the imminent death of his brother and by his strange advice my father left his side. Some hours later he returned to find that my uncle was being dressed in his royal robes of gold and his ceremonial jewels in preparation to attend his own funeral ceremony. Down to his ancestral temple in the courtyard, to the wailings and chantings of the court gathered below, the dying man was led and offerings were given to the gods, priests mumbled prayers, and cymbals clashed in a funereal dirge.

Just before the sun rose above the palace walls my uncle crumpled over the shrine and the leader of Jubbal was dead.

It was my first experience with death. Where had he gone? I begged to know. Why did he lie so pale and still? Just a few hours before I had heard his groans of pain and his cries for help. Now he was silent.

No one paid any attention to the small girl wandering blindly about the palace trying to understand what was happening. In their own grief they were far too busy to explain the end of life to me. "Run along and play," they said, "and don't bother us with your questions."

I stole quietly to my classroom and huddled on a small stool in the corner trying to figure things out for myself.

18

I was frightened when I thought of what had happened. If such a fate had befallen my uncle, leader of a state, a powerful man, what could happen to me, a slight girl who had no influence with anybody? I trembled in fear.

When my teacher entered the room I ran to him, tugging desperately at his robe, pleading with him to tell me why my uncle cried no longer. "He has gone to God," answered my teacher. "If he is pure enough in heart, he will remain there. In any case, my child, he is far happier now."

I stared at him in wonderment. "But if he is happier now," I said, "why does everyone weep?"

My teacher did not answer. He looked at me silently and went about his work. A few minutes later he lifted his head. "Someday you will know," he said.

Some hours later I heard them bustling about my uncle's room while I stood near the corridor in the way of everyone who hurried past. They were preparing his body for the traditional Hindu cremation which was to take place over an open fire on the banks of a small stream several miles away. After the body was burned the eldest son would break the skull to show it had been fully destroyed but, since the Rana's son was still a boy, my father would substitute.

I listened, cold with horror, as my brother explained the ceremony to me. To be burned by fire! Supposing, I thought frantically, he was not really dead, that it was all a mistake. Mistakes could happen. How could they be sure? I got up and started to run down the corridor. My brother followed me and caught hold of my arm.

I wrenched away. "I must go," I gasped, "I must stop

them at once." Then I walked around in a slow circle. In my heart I knew it was no use. No one would listen to me, a little girl. And in my heart I knew he was dead and gone from me forever.

In the weeks following, in the manner of children, I began to forget my uncle and even managed to stifle my own fears. The funeral and the terror faded into the past and now the sounds of weeping and wailing echoing through the palace bored me. "Why don't they stop?" I thought, wanting life to be the way it was before my uncle's death, but it never was again. For with his death my whole life changed.

The successor to the throne of Jubbal was my uncle's twelve-year-old son, but since he was too young to conduct affairs of state it was necessary to appoint a regent. In spite of his brother's deathbed advice, my father wanted desperately to be appointed regent for his nephew. But my uncle's wife was determined to rule for her son and was backed in this by her minister.

My father, a proud and sensitive man, was crushed by her refusal to allow him to participate in the governing of Jubbal and, remembering at last the words of my uncle, with sadness he prepared to leave his home. This decision to leave was heart-wrenching for him but he knew that it had to be done.

He approached the minister and my aunt with the request that he be given our share of the family treasure but they refused to discuss it with him. Finally he threatened my aunt, the Rani, with an appeal to the British government. Shortly afterward the minister committed expensive suicide by eating crushed diamonds mixed with poison and left a letter addressed to my father confessing that over a period of years he had used a large part of the funds with which he had been entrusted. My aunt was horrified by this news but was more determined than ever not to divide the remainder of the fortune.

There was much quarreling and anger inside the palace. My father felt righteously indignant; after all, he had been raised as a prince and knew no other life. The thought of making his own way was both upsetting and frightening to him. But my aunt grew more and more hostile, refusing any longer to listen to him and denying his right to share his family's fortune. Publicly she announced that our family would no longer be supported; our food supplies were to be cut off within a day or two.

Speechless with fury, my father decided to risk a public scandal by appealing openly to the British government, and ordered my mother to begin preparations for moving to the capital of Simla where he would make this appeal. With shouts of glee we children heard the news that we were going to accompany them. For us it was a glorious occasion, the first time we were leaving the palace walls to see the world outside.

For my mother it was a move filled with terror. All her life she had been sheltered and protected from the world outside. Now she was leaving her home forever. She wept in bewilderment, while we danced about in delight, wondering that there could be sadness in the wonderful adventure on which we were about to embark.

The journey from Jubbal to Simla was a long and tiresome one. My mother and the five of us children were carried on *palkees* (litters enclosed by silk curtains) by coolies while my father rode a hill pony. We were accompanied only by ten personal servants and a large number of coolies; my father's first wife and three children did not come with us to Simla—I never knew why, but they remained behind in the palace at Jubbal.

Our road was a mule track and it took us four days to travel the fifty-mile distance. Even with the overnight stops at rest houses along the way we sometimes wept with heat and exhaustion as our caravan wound its way up and down the dusty paths and the burning summer pressed down upon the silken curtains of our palkee.

We came upon Simla at night. As we rounded a curve in the rocky trail I pulled aside the curtains and saw for the first time in my life thousands of winking lights spilling down the black slope of the city. We had never seen electric lights before and stared in open-mouthed wonder at the fairyland before us. Now the long journey was forgotten and only the new and enchanting world lay ahead.

A dear friend of my father, the Maharaja of Kapurthala (who later became my father-in-law), lent us one of his houses during our stay in Simla. For the children, "Newlands" was a fascinating place if only for its electricity with which we endlessly experimented, turning lights on and off for the pure magic of seeing them work just once more. But our new home was also a more lonely place than the palace at Jubbal with its many playmates. Now I was more or less alone with my two sisters.

For my brothers Simla was far more exciting than Jubbal. As boys they were permitted to leave the house and often they were taken on trips through the exotic bazaars and noisy streets of Simla. But I was forced to remain at home, in purdah with my mother and sisters. I was heartbroken and bewildered by this. At last I had seen a glimpse of the world beyond the palace walls; now I was not allowed to enjoy it.

"What is so different about a girl?" I wept one day as my brothers dressed for an excursion into Simla. "Why *can't* I go with them? Why must I always stay here when I want so much to go?"

"It's not fair," I said to my mother, stamping my foot in anger. "I want to see the world, too!"

My gentle mother looked at me reproachfully and her eyes filled with tears. Sheltered as she had been in her childhood, retiring and docile, she could not begin to understand the black rebellion that filled my heart at these injustices. I could see no reason for keeping me locked up like a baby. I ran as fast as my brothers, I knew all their games, even won them occasionally, why then could I not be part of their adventures? Patiently, my mother tried to explain. But it was an impossible task. She had always accepted her role; to question it was sacrilege. In her world a woman did what was expected of her, uncomplainingly. She did not ask for the privileges of a man.

Now, at my early age, I was trying to defy convention. While I cried loudly my mother shook her head sadly and began to pray. Perhaps a power beyond hers could bring obedience into my heart.

After a while I stopped weeping and watched from the

balcony as my father and brothers made their way across the courtyard, laughing and joking as they walked toward the magic city I could not see. Once again I was defeated. But someday, I promised myself, I would not only see Simla, I would see the whole world. I clenched my fists on the railing and bit my lips to keep back the tears, but they came again in a flood. For I never expected that someday my promise would be fulfilled.

Meanwhile, my father pressed his lawsuit against the Rani. Unfortunately, the viceroy's government turned it over to the local Punjab authorities where my aunt had powerful friends among the officials and the most my father could obtain was a small pension. By this time he was angry and his prestige so badly wounded that he demanded official recognition of himself as sole regent during my cousin's youth. This was refused and, deeply humiliated, my father swore to pass the rest of his life in exile. He never did return to Jubbal.

As winter came upon Simla father arranged to take us to Hardwar, one of the sacred cities of India. My mother had longed to make a pilgrimage to the holy city and now she felt brave enough to make the journey. With her trip to Simla she felt that she had seen much of the world already.

Our trip to Hardwar meant my first taste of freedom and I was dizzy with it. We traveled this time by railway and, although we maintained strict purdah on the train in a separate compartment for women and children, I saw dozens of strange and unfamiliar faces. The noise and the dirt and the howling of babies were equally enchanting after the quietness of life at Simla. In rapture I drank it all in, trying not to miss a single thing, turning my head eagerly from side to side as the train lumbered up and down the dusty hills, staring at the brown huts along the way and the ragged Indian children who stared back at me with round dark eyes.

And Hardwar itself was even more exciting. Here I found dozens of children to play with and once again I shouted and raced and romped noisily. Here, too, most restrictions on women were relaxed because it was a holy city. Now I could walk beside my brothers and explore with them the crooked narrow streets of Hardwar.

We even went swimming, separated, of course, from the male sex. At Hardwar, swimming in the holy waters of the Ganges has a religious significance, but for me sinking into its cool unfathomable depths and splashing about in the waves was a purely pagan pleasure. After life in the mountains the sight of these rippling waters was endlessly absorbing. I loved to feel the water on my arms, dip my face in it over and over again to let its coolness slip down my cheeks, until my mother would chide me. "Foolish girl," she would say. But I did not care. I had found a new love and was happy.

In the evening as the twilight deepened over the tranquil Ganges and hundreds of worshippers chanted softly on its banks, each pilgrim who had come to Hardwar to find faith lit a flame in a small paper boat and set it afloat on the dark waters. Silently, I murmured my prayers as I watched the boats careen downstream, hundreds of tiny flames winking in the night before toppling over into the holy river.

We had been at Hardwar about three months when the Maharaja of Kapurthala made his request for my hand in marriage to his son, the Tika Raja. It was here that my mother wept and pleaded with my father not to permit this unholy alliance and it was here that she failed and my betrothal was arranged.

At the time of my engagement, many marriages then being arranged in India for children were consummated the moment both were physically capable, some even before the bride reached puberty. But our parents considered themselves extremely advanced. The Tika Raja and I were to remain apart, receive our educations, and marry at an appropriate age. My future was to be in the hands of his father, the Maharaja of Kapurthala, who would direct my education and upbringing. In other words, he was now my guardian. It was the end of my carefree childhood.

The engagement festivities took place in Kapurthala. There were parades with soldiers and elephants, feasts, dances, and fireworks. Hundreds of poor came from all directions to watch the excitement and receive coins and food. But I know this only from hearsay. I, the bride-to-be, was not allowed to see or participate in the celebrations. Again I was in purdah. But by now I was beginning to accept my lot and did not object. In a way, I was glad. Somehow I felt that if I stayed with the children I could protect myself from facing what was really happening. I was a happy child. I was not so anxious to grow up.

But all children like to receive presents. Precious silks, brightly colored embroideries were given me for my trousseau and from my father-in-law a small diamond ring and some antique jewelry. Privately I didn't think much of his gifts. With all the fuss being made I had expected something a little closer to a diamond tiara.

At the end of the winter I lived apart from my family for the first time. I was sent to Mussoorie, a hill city slightly smaller than Simla. There I was installed in a small house with my own servants, my ayah, and an English governess named Miss Marble. Some distance away, the Maharaja of Kapurthala lived in a large French chateau and my own family were also nearby.

My ayah was a great comfort to me and a difficulty at the same time. She reminded me of home and my old life and made me feel I was not alone with strangers. But she hated Miss Marble. I realize now that she was threatened by her. My ayah loved me and wanted to be first in my affections. Now she felt I would be influenced by this interloper.

I was torn between two worlds. I remembered with longing the warm, companionable life with my family and sometimes after seeing my brothers and sisters I would weep with loneliness. Alone in an unfamiliar house which echoed only the voices of my servants I would wander sadly through the rooms wondering if the ache which gnawed at my young heart would remain there always.

Miss Marble was the first European I had met. She was a thin, homely spinster who tried to be kind. But I could not understand her and she could not understand me. From the moment she met me she began to speak English. How strange the language sounded to my ears. How brittle and clipped after the soft, endless jabbering of Hindus. She seemed like someone from another world. And of course to me she was untouchable.

As a Hindu child I was raised to feel that contact with anyone from a lower caste than myself would contaminate me and prevent me from reaching the heights of my religion. But Miss Marble had no caste. She was a European, a complete alien. As such, she was more untouchable than the lowest Hindu untouchable.

My ayah reminded me of this constantly. She even tried to blame my illness that summer on the evil influence of this peculiar European. She mimicked Miss Marble, lurching stiffly about my room, making short harsh sounds with her mouth. She sneered and grumbled and complained constantly and most of the time I gladly agreed with her.

But gradually I became fascinated with Miss Marble's tales of the world outside my narrow gates, the life which went on outside that of India itself. She told me of Paris and London and the new and exciting land of America. She helped select European frocks for me. How wonderfully unfamiliar they felt swirling about my legs. And how much easier to walk and play in than our traditional sari.

"This is the way little girls in Europe look!" I shouted to my ayah as I twirled about in front of the mirror in my new frock. "Is it not wonderful?" I asked her excitedly.

"No, it is not nice," she said, and her face looked angry and sad at the same time. "And I do not like it."

But for once I did not agree with her. I liked it. Some of my old rebellion came back to me and life seemed adventurous once more. India was not the whole world, after all.

Maybe it would be fun to be a European. Perhaps some day I would find out for myself. And my spirits rose as I danced away from my ayah, giggling at her tears, and went to find Miss Marble to tell me some more stories of Europe.

But when I was ill it was to Ayah I turned once more. She comforted me endlessly, sat by my bed, and it was good and familiar to have her close by. Now I was distrustful of Miss Marble.

I was learning to eat my meals at a table like Europeans instead of Indian-fashion on the floor, but because of my mother's feelings about caste, and my own, I was permitted to eat alone with only my ayah present to serve me. One day, when I was still ill and fretful, Miss Marble, who was worried about me, came to my room to make sure the meal was suitable for an invalid.

I heard a step at the door and looked up. Miss Marble was standing at the entrance. Suddenly my stomach turned over. "You must not come in!" I shouted. But Miss Marble did not understand. She walked through the door.

Now I was all Hindu again and she was the alien, the untouchable who would contaminate me. "I told you not to come in," I sobbed and was violently and thoroughly sick all over the tablecloth.

My European education was far from complete.

Chapter Three

It was with a little English girl named Sheila —whose mother was a friend of Miss Marble and whose father was a colonel in the British Army, stationed nearby —that I began to understand the strange and curious ways of Europeans.

Perhaps all children, no matter how different the cultures from which they emerge, have helplessness as a bond between them in a world of giants who arrange their lives with such reckless tyranny. In this kind of sympathy the very young are sometimes drawn together as if to pit their weakness against the strength of incomprehensible adults. It was probably that and only that which drew Sheila and me together, for our only similarity lay in the fact that we were both small girls. In every other way we were completely different, in looks as well as in temperament.

At times Shelia exasperated me nearly to the point of

madness. Once, in a rage of anger, I seized her by the pale curls which tumbled about her delicate face and shook her until she howled with a noise as unladylike and scandalous as she believed me to be. It was true. I had very little desire to be a lady. I was bored beyond measure at having to sit still, and envied, with a large jealous pain in my heart, the excitement which seemed to me to be happening in a world which lay just outside my finger tips.

Sheila, on the other hand, was more than content to be a girl. She wanted to be just like her mother, a tall English beauty who drifted in at teatime with a large garden hat and swirls of white organdy floating about her. Sheila, always awed by her presence, would leap up from play to curtsy and kiss her mother on the cheek, staring all the while in disbelief at her beauty. I tried to be polite and would bow my head, but secretly I thought Sheila's mother dull and stupid and would stand first on one foot and then another as she asked her endless questions about what we were playing and why we were doing it. Now I see she was trying to be nice to us in the only way she knew how but then I felt strongly her pretended interest in what she obviously thought were trivial childish matters.

Sheila's favorite game was playing tea—I was bored to death by it but gave in occasionally in order to get her to play my games of climbing trees and attempting daring stunts which frightened her and sent the servants into a frenzy of screeching and threats. Sheila tried to be a plucky little girl and when it was her turn to play my way bravely allowed me to lead her into what she was sure was fatally treacherous. I must admit I was not nearly such a good sport when it came to playing tea.

In spite of our language barrier—Sheila could not understand one word of Hindustani and my English was only less than fair—she attempted to teach me, as she had been taught, the most complicated set of rules and etiquette regarding the drinking of tea. I, who by this time had my own servants, and had much made of me as the princess who would marry a maharaja, was incensed by any criticism or instruction, particularly from a little girl I secretly considered beneath me.

"You don't hold your cup nicely at all," she would say primly in her thin English voice. (Without understanding every word, I knew exactly what she was saying.)

"You must sit more like a lady. Like my mother, not like some rough little boy."

Because I had some sense of fairness I tried to play the game as she wanted me to but inside I was seething with resentment and hatred. One day her blue eyes grew round and her mouth pouted in delicate disdain as I splashed the water we pretended was tea onto Sheila's best pink-and-white cloth.

"My goodness," she said, pulling back from the table and clutching her starched, white pinafore to avoid getting wet, "don't you even know how to pour tea yet?"

Suddenly it was all too much. This dull, pale, little English girl telling me what to do, looking at me with disdain. I lost my temper completely. I planted my two feet on the ground, with my hands on my hips and with a cry of rage began shouting at Sheila in Hindustani. It mattered not at all to me that she couldn't understand a word I was saying. I was sick to death of being reproved by her. No one was going to tell me what to do!

"Yes," I said, screaming at her in Hindustani. "I know how to pour tea!" And with those words I took the pot of water and turned it upside down over her blonde curls.

Once more I had reduced my little friend to screams and tears as she sat there with the water dripping over her face and onto her clothes. But as the governesses rushed to the scene, I had not the slightest trace of repentance. Instead, I turned to my nurse and said haughtily, "You must take me home at once. I have been insulted here."

But in spite of my difficult ways and erratic behavior Sheila and I remained fast friends for the time she was at Dehra Dun. For Sheila, I was different and exciting; from Sheila I began to understand the ways and charms of the Western world.

Many happy days were spent in Dehra Dun without quarreling. The house which my future father-in-law had provided for me had a lovely garden, grown thick with dark trees and cool damp bushes, in which to run about and play. For the first time I was permitted to have pets to play with me and I could scarcely contain my joy at being allowed to choose all I wanted. Naturally, I didn't know where to stop and at once selected several cats, dogs, a golden pony, rabbits, mice, parrots, and chickens. For hours I amused myself by going from one to the other and having long conversations with all my animal friends. I was in many ways a lonely child, isolated at this time from my family and frightened by the future so constantly under discussion by the grownups about me. It was a great relief to have animals to talk to who would listen sagely with large dumb faces and never turn my words back to me in reproach.

At that time I fell very ill with dysentery and as I look back upon the cure, two tablespoonfuls of castor oil every two hours, I am amazed that I lived at all, let alone recovered in just a couple of weeks.

Soon after my illness there were many changes in the house at Dehra Dun. For one thing, my little friend Sheila left with her family to return to England. As much as I criticized her, plagued, and tormented her, I missed her very much and thought over and over again as I played aimlessly about the garden in my solitude that if she were to return I would treat her very well indeed, knowing in my heart that if I could wish her back in the garden with her big blue eyes and dainty dimity dress that only the briefest time would elapse before I would once again begin finding fault with her. Such are the empty promises made in loneliness.

When winter came that year my English governess, Miss Marble, was sent away and replaced by two new European governesses, Miss Piggott and a French woman named Mademoiselle Meillon. From the moment I saw her I loved Miss Piggott. By then, and mainly through Sheila, I had got used to what I considered the strange ways of the English and, although she had the typical British dignity and reserve, she was kind to me and amused me by telling small stories and jokes. I was more wary of Mademoiselle. Conventional and somewhat stiff, there was little humor in her and, furthermore, she considered my laughter and raucous behavior completely unbefitting a small princess. She showed her disapproval and I did not like it. Too, I knew that just before coming to me she had been governess to my future bridegroom, the Tika Raja, who was now at school in England. I was not so anxious to think about that part of my life or to be reminded of my forthcoming marriage.

As the hot, humid cloud of summer began to descend on us, preparations were made to remove us all to the cool mountainous country of Simla. My own family, too, came to escape the heat, but once again we were all installed in separate houses. Because of my position, my house was much larger than that of my parents, even though I, a lone little girl, was to occupy it solely with my servants. The house, called Ravenswood, was a square, wooden building, painted a dull red on the outside. Like all the houses and palaces I had ever lived in, inside it looked just the same. Although the floors were carpeted with rich and luxurious materials, hand-loomed by patient and skillful fingers, there was no furniture in the rooms. This was in strict accord with Indian custom. We sat on mattress-like mats on the floor and when extra guests came there were piles of brightly colored, woven cushions for them to sit on and small, square stools woven in cotton, colored ribbons to eat from. It was a simple way to live, and often, since those years, I have wished I could go back to the simplicity of my childhood. But the years abroad changed my concepts and I learned to find too much comfort in the complications of modern living.

Life in Simla was quite different from anything I had yet

known. Far from the isolation I had felt at Dehra Dun, every attempt was now made for me to mingle in the social world of Simla. I was encouraged to make friends with the European children and attended many of their parties. Gradually I began to lose some of the security I had known as a small, locked-in Indian princess. As exciting as the world about me seemed and as delighted as I was that the gates were opening at last, I was a little frightened as well. It was the beginning of the feeling of entering a world between two worlds, the start of my uncertainty as to whether I was to be of the East or of the West.

My first real love was an Englishman, Colonel Greene, Simla's civil surgeon, who was called in when my governess, Mademoiselle Meillon, fell ill. At once I lost my childish heart to him, perhaps only because he patted my cheek and smiled at me. Each time he left I immediately sat down and wrote him a note asking him to come again soon. But it was so difficult for me to write in English that I could only copy the wording of the letters I had written to my little friend, Angel Thompson. It must have been with some surprise that Colonel Greene received my laboriously written letters beginning with "My darling doctor" and ending with "much love and kisses, your Brinda."

Two of my favorite people were Irene and Cynthia Curzon, daughters of Lord Curzon, one of India's most famous viceroys. I saw little of him at that time but came to know Lord Curzon years later and to admire his courage and wisdom in his guidance of India. In those days I was far more interested in the wonderful parties given by Lady Curzon in the Viceregal Lodge for the children.

Actually, that year I was far too absorbed in myself and

my own problems to spend much time thinking about anyone else. I was busy, not only with lessons and manners, but I had my first taste of society and a world which moved in a whirl of parties and entertainment. And even at that age I could not help but be aware of the interest which was shown in me at Simla that season. As a young princess, engaged to the son of one of India's wealthiest maharajas, I was virtually an object of curiosity in a city, like all places, where not enough happens to prevent people from wanting to live other people's lives.

I pretended not to notice but I heard the whispering and the speculative looks as I entered a room. And from my own loneliness and uncertainty I wanted to see myself through the eyes of these strangers. I was glad to be the black-eyed princess walled in a big house, surrounded by servants and with a brooding prince in a far-off land who would come to carry me off. No greater fantasy has any spinner of fairy tales been able to create than I, as a little girl in Simla.

But a storm was gathering over my head and only a few weeks after I was established in Ravenswood my ivory tower nearly tumbled about me. It was by the sheerest accident that I even learned something was the matter. In the manner of parents, mine preferred to keep me in ignorance as much as possible.

Returning one day to their house in Simla to retrieve a book which I had left behind, I heard loud, angry voices coming from the sitting room. Over the din I recognized the sharp voice of my aunt, the Dowager Rani of Jubbal.

"It is an unsuitable match," she was shouting. "I cannot

permit such an insult to our family and to the Hindu faith!"

I heard my father answer her in a voice full of indignation and rage. "We have given our word," he said. "It is too late now for your protests."

"It is not too late for me," she threatened. "You shall see, I will have this marriage stopped at once!"

When I realized that I was the subject of this heated discussion I rushed into the room and pleaded to know what was happening. But my father did not answer me and my mother only wept. My aunt started to speak but my father silenced her. In anger she turned away and left the house.

It was impossible to learn the truth from them but some time later the whole story came out. My aunt, widow of my father's brother, the ruler of Jubbal, had been responsible for my father's plight in having to leave his home. Now, still jealous of the affection which once existed between them, she was trying to interfere once more in our lives.

My aunt was a princess of Delath and she claimed that she did not want to see the royal name of the Rajputs sullied by the lesser family of Kapurthala, since both my parents were related to the Rajput rulers of a number of states both in the hills and on the plains. Obsessed with the idea of stopping the marriage, she journeyed from one Rajput family to the other trying to stir up enough agitation to give her the needed support. Such a row resulted that the Punjab government called upon my father and tried to interfere. Nearly beside himself he ordered them from the house.

My aunt's plan was to take me away from Simla by force

and put me in the fort at Jubbal. I was not the least bit frightened by this idea since I had only the happiest memory of my days in the palace there. Instead, I regarded it as an adventure full of exciting possibilities. Now the princess was to be stolen from her castle and hidden away from the heartbroken prince. I had no worries about *him*. At that point he was less than a stranger to me.

In this spirit I tried to discuss the matter with my mother.

"Since you didn't approve of the match in the first place," I said carelessly, "perhaps it would be all for the best if we followed aunt's advice and abandoned the marriage."

My mother looked at me with an expression of amazement. "How can you suggest such a thing?" she asked and burst into tears.

Now I was confused as I tried to comfort her. It was only a short time ago that my mother wept because this marriage was to take place. Now she was weeping because it might not be consummated.

That night I lay awake and tried to understand what was happening about me. I realized that my mother, in the submissive way of Indian wives, had become not only reconciled to the match but had taken on the enthusiasm of my father. Furthermore, she hated my aunt for the pain she had caused us and was determined not to let her have her way. From that moment on she enthusiastically endorsed my marriage to the Tika Raja and took every opportunity to lecture me about my duties to the family and state of Kapurthala.

The incident, however, caused such a stir that talk buzzed about me for many months. Even the servants gossiped and once I overheard a conversation that made me rush back into my room in a flood of tears.

"The princess' family must allow the marriage," they were whispering. "They say that since they have had to leave Jubbal they are very poor. And the Kapurthala state would be a good match."

How dare they say such a thing, I thought. I knew such talk didn't originate with servants. They had heard it from the servants of other homes who listened to the conversations of their masters. I cried with humiliation. So those were the whispers that hushed about me as I entered a room. How dare they say such things about us? I was ill with indignation. There must be no truth in such vicious gossip. Yet, I never could bring myself to speak of the incident to my parents or had the courage to question them about the real state of our affairs.

My aunt's interference, however, was quickly dispensed with as soon as my future father-in-law, the maharaja, stepped into the picture. A man of enormous power and will, he would brook no meddling with his plans. I was never told exactly what he did to calm the storm about me but the Rajput opposition and criticism of my marriage was stopped. The whispering continued but no one dared to invite his wrath openly.

We remained in Simla over Christmas. My days were spent largely in the classroom with Mlle Meillon. But I was beginning to outgrow our makeshift classroom. There was a limit to the amount of education Mademoiselle could offer me. Furthermore, she was shocked at the lack of education available to children in India and was determined to see that I fared better, particularly since my future husband, the Tika Raja Paramjit Singh was soon to leave India to complete his education in England.

Mademoiselle began a long campaign of talks with the maharaja in an attempt to convince him to send me away to school. At first he was horrified at the very idea. Educate a girl in Europe? He believed that the concession he had made to modern times in supplying me with a French governess was more than could be expected of him and at first flatly rejected every argument she presented. But Mademoiselle was a clever woman of indomitable will who was determined to have her way. She cajoled and flattered him. What a feather in his cap, she suggested, for his son to marry a princess of noble blood who would also have the added distinction and social graces of a European education.

Perhaps he thought, too, that it would be wise to remove me from the influence of my family especially so soon after the conflict over my marriage and that his control over me would be greater if he alone planned my upbringing without any possibility of future interference.

So I was told that I was going away to school. I had no idea what this meant, picturing a room in a school much like the classroom in my own house. That I was to leave my family and India and all I had ever known never occurred to me.

Once again my poor little mother wept, this time with terror as well as sorrow, when she learned from the maharaja that my education was to be completed in France. Not only was she worried about my bodily health but she was torn apart by what she believed to be the utmost peril to my soul. In her orthodox belief, crossing the black water—as most Indians call the sea—involved an enormous loss of caste and danger to my spirit. For weeks she cried and entreated my father to prevent this catastrophe but he was persuaded by his friend, the maharaja, and there was nothing else for Mother to do but agree.

The snow was falling heavily in Simla the morning I kissed her goodby for the last time. I never saw my mother again. She died before I came back to India. But to the last moment, the day I set out for Kapurthala before my trip she was brave and did not tell me of the long journey which lay before me nor of what "going away to school" would really mean.

Back in Kapurthala Mademoiselle Meillon took over completely. Together we stayed in the guest house which was built by the maharaja for his European friends. Furnished completely in European style it was far different from the way I had been accustomed to living. But I was already willing to accept the new life before me and at once felt at home there.

About ten days before we were to leave India, Mlle Meillon called me into her room. In a grave voice she told me that I was to leave India for France to continue my education.

"Be brave," she said, "for you are a princess and must learn to expect that your life will be encumbered by duty and responsibility."

Be brave? I squealed with delight and impulsively hugged Mademoiselle about the waist. What could be more wonderful than to go to Europe? All the stories my former governess, Miss Marble, had told me about life in the Western world came flooding back to me. The dances, the pretty clothes, the longed-for freedom! Brave? I was in ecstasy at the very thought of the trip.

My ayah wailed and shook her head forebodingly. "It's a bad omen," she moaned, "a bad omen!" But I shouted in glee at her lamentations.

"I'm going to be a little European girl now," I teased, "and wear dimity dresses and dance all night!" My ayah wept in horror as I skipped out of the room to talk to Mademoiselle once more about our trip.

We travelled first to Bombay by rail where we boarded the P. and O. liner, *Caledonia*. The sight of the enormous liner made me gasp with wonder. It was like a whole city. Exclaiming with excitement I rushed about the ship trying to examine it all at once.

On the boat for the first time, I saw what life was like for girls who lived in societies without restrictions. Mlle Meillon, as conventional as she was, was European-bred and was relieved that at last I was out of purdah and could mingle with people who, a few days back, I would have had to regard as untouchable.

The news that a young princess was allowed her first taste of freedom probably had much to do with the warm kindnesses shown to me on the *Caledonia* and I enjoyed every moment of the trip, playing deck games all day long and winning first prize in a pillow-fighting contest which was held at the end of the voyage. How my mother and Ayah would have wept in horror at the loss of caste involved as I hurled pillows across the deck! But then I did not look back. I was busy learning to have a life of my own.

Had I been my grandmother I might have worshipped the electric fan in my cabin. As it was, the whirring fan and cool breeze which blew from it kept me fascinated, particularly when I was confined to my cabin because the hot Red Sea rolled and my poor head wobbled with seasickness. The cool breeze then was my only comfort, as I doubted for a few days that I had ever been meant to live such a reckless life. But once my stomach settled and my head stopped rocking, my spirits came back and I raced once more around the deck with abandon.

Mademoiselle and I watched the sunset spill its gold over the Suez Canal and then we were at Port Said where, perched high on the deck, I watched with fascination the unloading of cargo by natives on the dock.

Then, sooner than I would have believed possible, it was early morning and we were in France. Shivering in my thin nightgown, I hurried to the porthole and watched the fairyland of Marseille emerge from the blueness of the dawn. Suddenly the clouds parted and the sun burst through. My heart pounded. My new life had begun.

Chapter Four

We drove by horse-and-carriage from the docks at Marseille to the fashionable Hotel du Louvre, my head twisting from side to side trying to take in all the sights as Mademoiselle admonished me to sit still like a nice young lady.

The few days we spent in Marseille before going on to Paris were spent in wandering about the city shopping and sight-seeing, and Mademoiselle visited the Notre Dame de la Garde where she lit a candle and said a prayer of thanksgiving for our safe journey.

The day before we left Marseille we lunched with friends of Mlle Meillon's in a residential section of Marseille, and I had my first lesson in the problems of European living.

In my eyes my manners were perfect. Had I not spent long, torturous hours with several governesses practising how to sit at a dinner table, use the strange implements of the Western world, and conduct myself as a young lady?

But I discovered that social conduct is a complicated and unpredictable thing.

It was a delicious luncheon and I ate well with the hearty appetite of youth. I couldn't help glancing, however, even as I ate, at the large silver dish in the center of the table, piled high with ripe, fresh fruit. Such fruit was scarce in India. My mouth watered each time the centerpiece caught my eye.

At the end of the meal the hostess offered me the bowl of fruit.

I smiled with pleasure. "Thank you," I said, remembering my manners. "Such lovely-looking fruit!"

Happily I began peeling a large pear. Then I happened to glance at Mademoiselle Meillon. She was looking at me crossly as if I had done something wrong. What could it be?

Perhaps I was eating too fast. Remembering her admonitions to "eat slowly and carefully" I chewed solemnly on the fruit. Then I realized that I was the only one eating fruit. Everyone else had declined and sat waiting until I had finished.

Then it was bad manners to accept the offer of fruit? I nearly choked in embarrassment but since I had already begun eating the pear I knew that all I could do would be to finish it with as much grace as possible, with the eyes of all the guests fixed upon me. It seemed to take forever to eat the pear and by this time, blushing with shame, it had lost all its flavor for me. I could have been chewing on a piece of wood.

"But why, Mademoiselle," I asked when we were back in our hotel room, "why do these Europeans offer fruit and not expect you to eat it?"

"Such fruit is a luxury," she answered impatiently. "It is just politeness for a hostess to offer it. And only piggishness," she added, "for you to accept it."

I sighed in bewilderment. Would the rest of my life be spent in confusion? I hoped Paris would be easier to understand.

I loved Paris from the moment we stepped off the train into the bustling crowds at the Gare de Lyon and drove through the winding little streets in a small, electric car to the home of the maharaja's friend, the Comtesse du Bourg de Bozas, where I was to be her guest for the first month or so of my stay.

Everything delighted me. The women, strolling along the Champs Élysées looking in shopwindows, seemed so happy; old men and fat nurses with children sitting in the parks gossiping, to me looked contented. For me Paris was full of joy and gaiety and as we drove up the wide avenue to the countess' home, the sun glittering on the Arc de Triomphe, I was thankful to the fate that was responsible for setting me down in this magic city.

The house of the Du Borg de Bozas in Rue Pierre Charron was probably typical of that wealthy, aristocratic society of Paris, but very different from houses I had known. I was enchanted by the furnishings, the giant crystal chandeliers which twinkled on the winding staircases and throughout the house, the thick, red carpeting, and the delicate, antique furnishings. There seemed to be so much furniture! From the starkness of India's barely furnished rooms I had stumbled into a museum of objects.

The countess was a genuinely hospitable woman who welcomed me affectionately and did her best to make me feel less of a stranger. She had four children, two daughters and two sons, all younger than I, who watched me all through tea with round, curious eyes and never said one word. But after tea when I followed them up to their nursery and we were left alone with their old, familiar governess, they screeched and romped and threw pillows at each other until I, dissolved in laughter, felt as at home as I had with the children in India.

For the next days the countess and Mlle Meillon spent most of their time trying to decide where my education would be best continued. The maharaja, realizing how much greater her experience was in such matters, had entrusted the choice to the countess with the help of Mlle Meillon. Since I was to have no voice in the decision, I had no interest in the discussions and spent my time with the children, visiting the zoo in the park and sight-seeing about a city I loved more dearly every day.

One morning Mademoiselle hurried into my room.

"There will be no sight-seeing today, young lady," she said briskly.

I opened an eye full of sleep and pulled the covers up to my neck.

"Is it time to get up already?" I sighed.

Mademoiselle's wrinkled face was full of smiles.

"It's all been decided," she said. "We have found a fine school for you."

"Just a minute more, Mademoiselle," I said, and turned over and fell fast asleep again.

I was awakened some time later by much scolding and shaking from Mademoiselle. It was necessary that I dress at once or we would be late for our interview with the headmistress of the school. They wanted to look me over to see if I would be a suitable student. This had an ominous sound.

L'Ascencion was an exclusive Parisian convent where French society girls had been educated for many years. As we drove through the winding drive, the buildings seemed dark and gloomy and for the first time since I had left India I felt a cold chill of terror. Living with such strangers as a boarding student, I realized suddenly, would be far different from the loving care lavished on me by our friends.

The tears were close to my eyes when we entered the office of the headmistress. She was a tall, stern woman who looked at me coldly and asked me a number of questions about my past education. As she reviewed what I had learned from my governesses it seemed pitifully inadequate and shame swept over me for having neglected my studies.

I tried not to show my fears as we walked through the dormitories and bit my lips to stop from crying. The school seemed to me to be a terrible prison where girls in uniform walked quietly about. I realized some time later that it was the presence of the headmistress which had subdued them but at the moment I could only surmise that I, too, would spend the next years of my life locked in this dark prison.

When we returned to the headmistress' office she gave

me what she must have considered was a kindly smile. In reality it was a grimace which twisted her face and made her seem many times more terrifying.

"Well, dear," she said, "how do you like L'Ascencion?"

I tried to speak but no words came. Behind me Mademoiselle pinched my arm.

"Why don't you answer nicely?" she said.

I looked first at the countess and then at the headmistress. My lips quivered. Still I could not answer.

"Speak up, my girl," said the headmistress briskly.

The countess, embarrassed by my silence, spoke for me. "I'm sure Brinda will be very happy here," she said.

When I heard those words I could not keep the tears back another moment. I opened my mouth to speak, to make excuses as politely as I could, but all that came out was a great howl of pain. Once I started I could not stop, but wept hysterically, my head buried on the countess' lap.

Finally, I stopped crying enough to speak. "It is a dreadful place," I cried between sobs. "I cannot live in such a prison."

The headmistress' mouth fell open at my words. She was not accustomed to such talk from well-bred girls. But I was at a point of desperation where nothing mattered but that I leave that school at once never to return.

The countess apologized for my behavior and we prepared to leave. But the headmistress was still angry at what she considered my impertinence.

"In any case," she said, (knowing there was no chance that I would come to her school) "we would not consider her a suitable student."

50

So my scholastic future was still undecided. The maharaja, however, had just arrived in Paris with his sons and we had a chance to discuss the problem with him. It was finally decided that I was to remain with the countess until autumn, then I would spend the next few years with some friends of hers who had agreed to accept me as a paying guest and send me to a day school with her daughters. I danced with relief. Now I would not be locked up in some gloomy boarding school but would be free to enjoy a home life with French girls my own age. It was a lovely prospect.

During the maharaja's visit I saw my fiancé for the first time since I was ten years old. With my governess and his two brothers, we walked in the Bois. I was curious to find out what he was like.

"Are you fond of school?" I asked him, not knowing quite what else to say.

"Not especially," he answered, looking down at the ground with a serious face.

"Isn't Paris fun?" I asked eagerly.

"Yes, it's all right," he said, still not looking at me nor changing what seemed to be a rather gloomy expression.

"Do you miss India?" There must be something he will talk about, I thought.

"No," he said abruptly and walked away.

Well, I thought, he's not much fun to talk to. But I didn't care. I turned to his brothers who were laughing and teasing each other and we had a gay time for the rest of the walk. But the Tika Raja walked alone and did not join in our merriment.

Paris, in those days, was at its height as the social capital of the world. And my hosts were among the few in its closed circle of society. The Maharaja of Kapurthala was accepted there, too, and as a result my welcome had been guaranteed from the start. There was some difficulty at first in fitting me into the right group, but the French with their Gallic charm decided that since I was engaged there was no reason for not having me participate in social gatherings suited to my premarital status rather than to my own age group.

In the five years that followed I made the most of my opportunity. I loved parties and excitement and relished every moment of fun and gaiety. I had a certain snob value of my own as a royal princess engaged to the heir of a romantic and wealthy domain. Everyone I met fussed over me and I cannot say I did not like it.

Yet even then as a young girl and constantly chaperoned, just beginning to learn about life, I was able to see that much of the flattery and fuss had very little to do with me as a person. Everyone was kind but I saw that they were being kind to Princess Brinda, wife-to-be of the heir of Kapurthala. It was a feather in their cap to entertain me, to boast about giving a dinner party or ball for the social success of the season. They were not nearly as interested in me as in raising their social prestige.

But this realization did not stop my enjoyment of the parties. I was still thrilled by flattery. All that had happened was that I ceased to believe in it or to think that I could find some answer to life in such attentions.

I was beginning to acquire a good deal of social confidence. In fact, often I was close to being more social than the Almanach de Gotha.

Once at a large, formal dinner party given in my honor

I almost gained the reputation for being something of a wit. Urged by my friends to wear Indian dress for the occasion instead of my usual European frock, I dressed in my most glittering sari with the thin, tinsel-like, gold cloth draped about me. Like a well-brought-up Indian girl, I was quiet and modest all through dinner, omitting this time my usual laughter and jokes. I fluttered my eyelashes to the table and answered only when spoken to.

I was acting a part and enjoying every minute of it. I was about as decorous as it is possible to be. Only one of my close friends glanced at me curiously and giggled as if she knew exactly what I was doing. But I paid no attention to her looks and kept my head slightly bowed.

But I was far too mischievous to leave the table with such a good impression. At the end of the meal the butler offered me some strong, highly flavored cheese, a custom unlike any in India where such smells are considered unappetizing.

I sniffed at the cheese loudly, twinkled my eyes at my host, and in a loud clear voice exclaimed, "Monsieur, why is it that you spoil a good meal with such smelly stuff?"

For a moment he looked shocked. But all the guests laughed loudly and he soon joined in. For such behavior in India I should have been punished; in France I was praised for my spirit and sense of humor.

Before it was time to leave the Du Bourg de Bozas, I suffered a severe attack of appendicitis and was sent to a nursing home for an operation. Before the operation took place I howled with pain and fright but as soon as it was over I was delighted at the enormous amount of attention paid to me. Flowers, books, and visitors deluged the room and I sat in the center of it, almost hoping it would never end.

At that time the daughter of the last Emperor of Brazil and wife of a French prince, her Imperial Highness Comtesse d'Eu, visited me in the hospital. A charming old lady, she was then over seventy years old but was still a lively and warm person. She brought as a present a Catholic Bible and a picture of the Virgin and Child.

"I do not know what your faith is, my child," she said, kissing me gently on the forehead, "but I do know that the same God looks after all little children everywhere." I have always kept that picture with me; it still hangs above my bed.

The time had now come to leave my first Parisian friends. It was autumn and school was about to begin. It was necessary for me to move into my new home and get settled before the duties of school would occupy me too much.

My new home was with the Comtesse de Pracomtal. She was a tall, stately, beautifully gowned Parisian woman who at first inspired me with awe. But, as with the Comtesse du Bourg de Bozas, her kindness wore away my initial shyness and I soon felt at home with her and the four De Pracomtal children.

There were two girls in the family, Beatrix, who was exactly my age, and Yolande, who was a few years older. Together the three of us went as day boarders to a school not far from our house and I began to feel a part of the De Pracomtal household. I was in a real family again at last.

For the moment my days of luxury and party-going seemed to be over. We were living a quiet life of school and study. Beatrix and I did not return home from the school each day until five o'clock; then from seven to eight we did our homework, changed for dinner with the grown-ups at eight-thirty, and again at nine-thirty were finishing up our work before bedtime.

Now more was expected of me mentally than ever before. Added to the burden of learning a foreign tongue and living in a country where all the customs seemed strange and peculiar to me, I was forced to concentrate on learning about ten times as much as I had in my small classroom in India. My curriculum in school included four languages: French, English, German, and Italian, elocution, painting, drawing, dancing, singing, piano, guitar, and mandolin, as well as sewing, knitting, embroidery, and the three R's. It was little wonder that I was bewildered and that for two years my grades were low.

The girls made fun of me for my stupidity. But since I myself had no respect for learning and much preferred to play jokes and have fun, they soon got tired of teasing and joined in playing pranks on the teachers. I was unscrupulous enough to take advantage of the teachers, knowing that since I was a princess they would not deal with me severely.

But as the annual examinations drew near, I began to worry. I realized with dismay that I had learned practically nothing at all since school had started and had wasted my time in foolishness. Now the time had come to pay for my frivolity and procrastination.

Myself at eight. Despite my demure appearance I could outclimb and outrun my brothers.

Here is my paternal grandfather, Rana Karam Chand, holding a rose!

Johnston and Hoffman

After the death of my uncle, Rana Padam Chand of Jubbal (left), my father (right) was exiled.

The wedding procession—on foot and on elephants—enters the palace gates.

Our Sikh marriage ceremony. The priest under the canopy is reading from the Sikh sacred book, the Granth-Sahib.

And this is the Old Fort, formerly the royal residence.

This more imposing building is the palace of the Maharajah of Kapurthala.

Myself in the mid-twenties.

The European guests at the wedding. My husband and I are in the second row center.

The large palace was too small to accommodate all the wedding guests, so this tent city was erected to take care of the overflow.

This beautiful white house was our wedding gift from my father-in-law, the Maharajah.

My husband, the Maharajah of Kapurthala.

Hay Wrightson, Ltd.

Princess Indira, my eldest daughter.

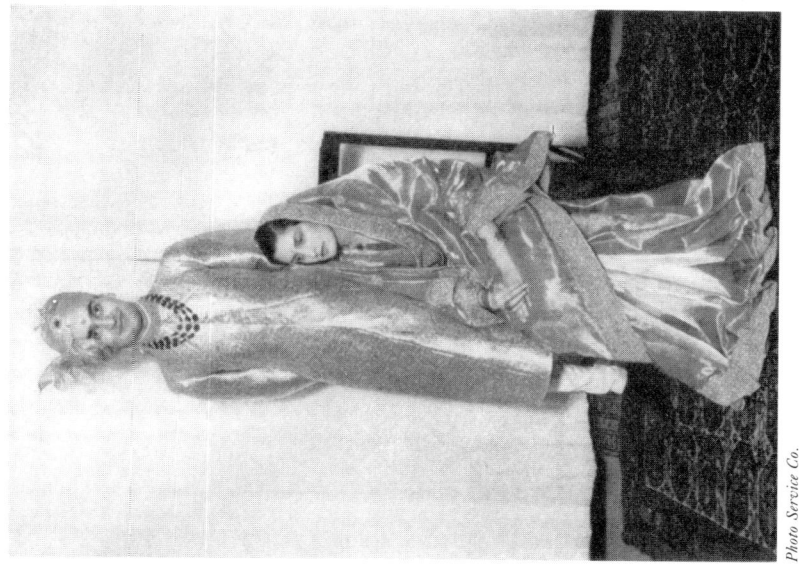

Princess Ourmila, my youngest daughter, at her wedding to Raj Kumar Berendra Singh of Jubbal.

Photo Service Co.

Wedding picture of my daughter, Princess Sushila, and Rajah Girraj Singh of Bharatpur.

My first grandson! Kanwar Arup Singh, son of Princess Sushila and nephew of H. H. Marajah of Bhra Bharatpur Kanwar of Bharatpur.

. . . And his younger brother, Anun Singh.

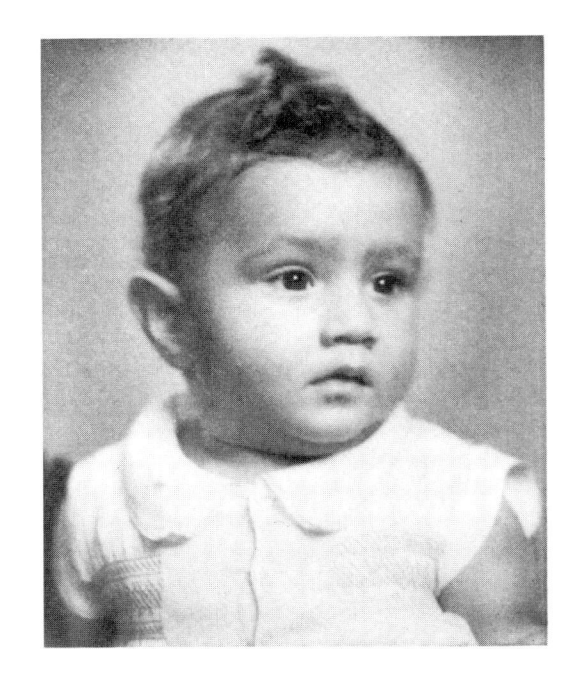

Kanwar Arup Singh with his cousin Kumari Neira of Jubbal, daughter of Princess Ourmila.

My third grandson: Udey Singh of Jubbal, son of Princess Ourmila.

Here I am, in 1922, with the Prince of Wales, later Edward VIII and then Duke of Windsor.

These formidable-appearing gentlemen are state officials of Kapurthala.

My father-in-law as he inspected his palace guard, only partially protected from the sun.

Associated Press Photos

In India with Pandit Nehru. I am on the far left.

Pio Campas Samanez

... And with the Brazilian Ambassador in Peru in 1953.

Coming down the staircase at the Brazilian Embassy in Lima. The Peruvian press reported: ". . . Princess Brinda looked like a golden goddess descending from Heaven." At my age that is the most charming and romantic compliment anyone could pay!

I was also too vain to want to appear stupid any longer to my classmates. I did not want their derision. I wanted to be praised and admired. So I made up my mind that somehow in two months I would make up for wasted time. For the next weeks I studied in every spare moment, devoting more than twice the usual amount of time to my homework. For the moment I put aside the joys of my practical jokes and settled down earnestly to try to make amends.

The result was that I actually won prizes in three subjects. However, in all the others I failed completely. Not only that, but since I was so anxious to pass I cheated during the examinations. Here fate played me her usual trick and I learned that nothing in life comes easily. For although I copied the answers from the other girls' papers, since I knew so little about the subjects the answers I copied had nothing at all to do with the questions. My cheating was discovered, and punished, but my biggest punishment was always the recollection of my stupidity in believing the rules of life did not apply to me.

It was difficult to struggle against the language problems. I had been forced several times already in my short life to switch from one language to another. First as a young child, I had had to learn English; now in my early teens I was expected to speak, learn, and think in French, and keep up with a class of more than seventy girls.

During these months Comtesse de Pracomtal had become my guardian and was now responsible for my welfare. I respected and admired her and felt happy to be treated as a daughter in her household. But after several months of this arrangement Mlle Meillon began to resent it bitterly.

Although I was fond of her, she was an extremely controlling woman and could not brook any interference by the *comtesse*. Mademoiselle loved me but the friction in the household began to increase and it was agreed by all of us that the best solution would be for Mademoiselle to leave. Although I missed her, in many ways it was a good thing. After that I learned to become more self-reliant.

For the first time in my life I was allowed to visit the theater. It was a magic discovery. As often as possible I went to the *Comédie Française* where I sat, holding my breath with excitement in the dusk as the curtain slowly went up. Oh, the wonder of the theater for a young girl. I would be a great actress, I decided, and someday the deafening applause and the shouts of "bravo" would ring for me. Brave, handsome men would fall in love with me and adore me, little children would run after me in the streets to touch the hem of my skirts. Such were my adolescent fantasies.

I practiced in the mirror, copied the gestures of the actress I had seen at that week's matinee, and recited endlessly not only to the mirror but to anyone who would listen.

Yolande, who was older than I, often listened patiently to my recitations. She said she liked to hear them but perhaps she was only being kind. Beatrix made no effort to be polite.

"Oh, Brinda," she would say crossly. "Let's do something else. It's no fun to listen to you being silly."

But no amount of criticism could arrest the burning desire I had to be an actress. I longed to act in a real play before a real audience. My opportunity came in my second year in France.

I spent the month of October that year in a fairy-tale chateau which belonged to Princess Amedee de Broglie, who had visited in India many years ago. When she met me in France she took me to her bosom at once and loved me because she had loved India so much. That October she invited me to spend the month at her castle, Chaumon-sur-Loire, where more than seventy guests were staying.

Knowing that I loved the theater, she arranged for several of the guests to present a one-act French play and awarded me the leading role. I was intoxicated with excitement. Here was the chance I had been waiting for.

The guard room of the castle had been converted into a theater and nearly three hundred people were gathered there to watch us perform. I was in an ecstasy of delight. My leading man was not only dark and handsome, he was one of French society's most popular amateur actors, Baron Henri de Bermingham.

I was dressed in the long gowns of the Princess' daughter-in-law, Princess Albert (who died young and tragically some years later at the age of twenty-six). But that night everyone was gay. My hair was up for the first time and I swept about the room I used for a dressing room, archly glancing over my shoulder at myself in the mirror and twirling about the room to watch the Princess' satin skirts whirl around me. I was full of confidence.

But as I came out of the room and prepared to go onto the stage my heart sank. From behind the curtain I could hear the noises of the hundreds of people waiting to see me. I listened to the hum and my courage fled. How dared I, little girl that I was, think that I could get up before this sophisticated audience accustomed to the magnificent talent of the French theater? My face turned scarlet in my embarrassment at my presumption.

The baron walked towards me. His uniform glittered in the dim light. He was dressed in a costume of a French officer. Once more I was struck with awe by his good looks and magnificent carriage. I felt more like a gauche little girl than ever.

I turned to him and clutched his arm in pleading.

"I'm sick," I whispered, scarcely able to speak, "I can't go out there."

The baron cupped my face in his slender hands and tilted it up to him. He looked in my eyes long and searchingly.

"You are not sick, my dear child," he said kindly. "You are nearly frightened to death."

I nodded dumbly.

"It is not easy to be a princess," he continued. "Nor is it easy to be anything. One must go blindly forward with only courage as a guide."

At that moment I had no courage. My eyes filled with tears.

"You are a charming child," the baron said. "People will love you—if you let them."

Then he took my hand in his and kissed it. "It is not bad to be frightened," he said, "only to let it run away with you."

I scarcely had time to think about his words. The curtain

had risen and the guests were applauding. Together the baron and I hurried onto the stage.

We were a huge success. My confidence came back and I felt inspired by the baron's acting. I was myself once more and lived the magic of the lovely lady whose part I was playing.

But most of all, I remembered the gentle words of the baron who tried to tell me that the most important thing in life is to believe in yourself.

Chapter Five

The theater was not enough for me. I wanted to do everything. And next on my list was horses.

I was determined to be a good horsewoman. My opportunity for that came quickly enough, for Princesse Amedee's house parties were famous for her stag hunts. It was fast, exciting riding and I was just learning to crush down the terror which flooded me as the horse galloped away when I had an accident. My pony tripped on one of the hounds and broke the dog's tail. My hostess forbade me to ride again.

She was worried, she said, that I would be hurt while in her care but her children giggled and said it was because she didn't want to see all her hounds with broken tails.

My next attempt at riding ended even more disastrously, on a visit to the country home of my old friends the Du Bourg de Bozas. They were not anxious for me to ride their horses because they were high-strung, racing animals. But I teased and begged and assured the *comte* that I was not only an adequate horsewoman but a brilliant one as well.

Dubiously shaking his head, the *comte* allowed me to mount one of his famous racing horses. I knew this horse was celebrated for his nasty temper as well. But flushed with confidence I settled into the saddle and flicked him lightly with my riding crop.

The horse reared violently. And while the Comte du Bourg de Bozas stood watching in horror, I was flung into the air, landing on my head. When I woke up I was in the soft white bed in my room with a bad concussion.

But still I could not give up. Back in Paris I begged to take lessons from the famous Irish horsewoman, Mrs. Huntsman. She was an excellent equestrienne and taught me well and I rode with her for two seasons. By the end of this time my confidence had come back and I felt I could handle any horse.

Then one day, riding a new horse in the Avenue des Accassias, the horse bolted and ran away. Half-hanging off the saddle, I tried to cling to his neck as he ran for nearly two miles before colliding with a tree near the crossing of the Avenue du Bois. The poor animal was stunned with the shock of the collision but I hung on, and was full of pride that although I lost my stirrups, hat, and whip, I didn't lose my head in that nightmare gallop.

I had lost my nerve, however, and never since that day have I ever sat on a horse with any assurance.

After that I decided I was not meant to be an athlete of

any great stature and turned again to more feminine pursuits.

At this time the De Pracomtals entertained constantly and the house was filled with the great figures of the day. Some of these famous people I met; some were names I heard gossiped about at the dinner table. Emile Zola, Marcel Proust, Sergei Diaghilev (who was considered a kind of unofficial ambassador of the arts from Russia although his Ballet Russe had not yet come to Paris), Dreyfus, and others were entertained lavishly by society and when they were not being entertained they were being talked about.

The French writer, Paul Bourget, once paid me one of the nicest compliments I have ever received. As he entered the drawing room of the De Pracomtals, Bourget fixed his monocle and asked the entire group, "Who is that charming young person who is pale like the day and black like the night?" I blushed profusely but later enjoyed a long conversation wherein he lectured me on French literature.

The *grande dame* of French royal society at that time was the Comtesse d'Eu, the old lady who had visited me in the hospital and given me a picture of the Virgin and Child. Born a princess of the house of Braganza, she had married into that of Bourbon and now ruled society like an old queen. That there was now a republic in France was a taboo subject. The president and ministers were never invited or even mentioned in the homes which comprised society. Royalty refused to recognize that Louis XIV was no longer in Versaille.

I remember well the first time I visited Count and

Countess d'Eu. Particularly since I was made to wear what was supposed to be my best afternoon frock. Actually I loathed the dress and protested bitterly against wearing it. But Countess de Pracomtal insisted. It was a pale blue taffeta dress with thousands of frills and tucks. The fussy style was unbecoming and the color turned my skin a greenish yellow. I was miserable in the dress and sulked all the way to the countess' house.

But as we entered the house I was introduced to the countess' two young sons, Prince Antoine and Prince Louis de Bourbon-Orléans. Feeling miserably inadequate in my hated dress, I barely spoke to the two young men. But they were gay and full of cheerful talk. They like me, anyway, I thought in amazement, in spite of my dress and the way I look. I was still insecure enough to believe that clothes could make such a difference.

I think Antoine knew how shy and ill at ease I felt for soon after we were introduced he drew me aside.

"Shall I tell you a funny story?" he said smiling.

"I'm not a child," I answered indignantly. "You don't have to amuse me by telling me stories."

"My," he said in surprise, "you're a touchy one, aren't you?"

Suddenly I was ashamed. He was trying to be nice to a shy, gauche girl and I was rebuffing him.

I smiled at him as nicely as I could, asked his forgiveness, and listened to his story.

His father, the count, it seemed, was extremely nearsighted. Not only that, but in his old age his memory had begun to fail. It was an arduous ordeal, therefore, to attend the many receptions and parties given by the countess since not only was he unable to remember their friends, but he could not see them with his weak eyes.

As a result, during the parties he would constantly run out of the drawing room into the entrance hall to consult the visitors book. Sometimes he took so long to figure out the names of the new arrivals that long lines of guests had to wait in embarrassment behind his stooped figure.

Naturally, the countess was often quite upset over it. She lectured the count severely but it was to no avail.

"What can I do, my dear?" he would answer her pleadingly. "If I cannot remember the names of your guests, they will be insulted."

Antoine and Louis, hearing so much talk and quarreling about this, decided to take the matter into their own hands and cure their father of rushing back and forth to the visitors book.

One evening, while their father was in the drawing room with all the guests, they sprinkled sneezing powder onto the opened pages of the visitors book. Then they waited quietly behind a huge palm tree in the marble hall. In a few minutes the count bustled out to peek at the book and with his nearsighted eyes bent his face down close to the pages. A violent explosion of sneezes shook the hall.

The old count staggered away, muttering to himself about devils and witchcraft. He never suspected his two mischievous sons of this deviltry but was convinced that the visitors book had become bewitched. After that he avoided it completely.

When Antoine finished telling me the story I laughed and laughed until tears came to my eyes. I forgot all about my ugly dress and my sulking because I didn't get my own way in delight at this lovely story of naughtiness. Immediately I became fond of Antoine and our love of mischief created a bond of friendship between us which was only broken years later when, like so many other young Frenchmen, he was killed after the outbreak of the first world war. But at that moment Antoine and I were very much alive as we entered the drawing room of his mother together.

I curtsied to his mother and the old lady kissed me and motioned me to a chair beside her. Just before I sat down I saw behind her chair an enormous portrait of her father, the late Dom Pedro, dressed in scarlet robes and white satin knee breeches.

The talk at teatime was dull and the guests chattered on interminably. My mind was not on the conversation. I tried not to think about Antoine because I knew it was improper to think about a young man, especially for a young woman who was already engaged. I concentrated instead on the picture behind the countess' head. But since I was sitting next to her it was very difficult to turn around to gaze at her imperial father without seeming to be rude. All I could manage to achieve were a few side glances now and then but as I was trying not only to stop thinking about Antoine but also to avoid listening to the dull talk, I kept twisting my head over my left shoulder.

The result was that from that visit my chief mementos were a pain in my stomach from letting the countess stuff me with sweets and cakes, and a pain in the neck from trying to look at the portrait of the last emperor of Brazil.

Another of our royal neighbors in Paris was the Grand Duke Paul of Russia. He had been exiled from Russia by the czar because after the death of his first wife he had made a morganatic marriage. He and his wife, the former Countess Hoenfelssen, lived only a few doors from us and Beatrix and I often played with their three children, Irene, Nathalie, and Vladimir.

Although Vladimir was only nine years old he looked like fifteen and was one of the handsomest boys I have ever seen. He was in love with me, he told me passionately, and although I could scarcely return such affection he pursued me constantly, rushing down the street on his bicycle and ringing the bell impatiently until I came into the garden and talked to him through the railings.

Countess de Pracomtal was furious when she learned of Vladimir's silliness and immediately had a long, serious talk with his mother who forbade him to continue in this fashion. Regretfully, he apologized but did not give up, and every Thursday he came to tea to our house with his mother.

I couldn't help liking him, he was such a charming little boy with a kind of intuitive fascination for women rarely seen in grown men.

"I insist you learn Russian," he would say, trying to sound grown-up and authoritative. "It is absolutely essential!"

Then I would giggle at his presumption and chuck him under the chin.

"Don't you think I know enough languages, Vladimir?" I would ask. "I can barely remember the ones I already know."

"At least let me teach you one sentence," he begged,

"What is so difficult about learning one little sentence?"

Laughingly I relented and every Thursday I would practise rolling the unfamiliar sounds over my tongue. Sometimes Vladimir would burst into gales of laughter at my clumsy attempts to learn his sentence.

"I'm not going to practice any more," I would say crossly when he giggled at me.

Then he would beg and coax and cajole me into continuing.

Sometimes Countess de Pracomtal would come into the garden where we were laughing and say, "What is it that you find so absorbing? Whatever are you children doing?"

Then Vladimir would draw himself up and say proudly, "Why, I am teaching her to speak Russian."

Shaking her head in amazement that two youngsters could occupy themselves so profitably, particularly when she knew my aversion to study, the countess would nod in approval and go back to her tea.

But Vladimir, although he hounded me into learning his sentence (an accomplishment I think I finally performed complete with a good Russian accent) would not tell me what the sentence meant.

"How can I ever use a sentence in Russian if I don't know what it means?" I asked him. "Perhaps I would say good morning to someone when it is really evening. There is no point to learning a language if it doesn't make any sense to you."

Vladimir laughed. "Oh, what do you care what it means?" he said. "You say it as nicely as a Russian princess."

But I was determined to learn what the sentence meant. One day when I was returning a visit to Vladimir's mother with the Countess de Pracomtal, I marched up to the Grand Duke.

"Vladimir has taught me some Russian," I said, "but he won't tell me what it means. Will you?"

The Grand Duke smiled. "I will do my best, my dear, to translate it."

Behind the Grand Duke I saw Vladimir gesturing frantically at me. His lips were moving silently. "Don't say it," he was trying to tell me, "don't say it."

But I was going to end the mystery once and for all. I stood squarely in front of the Grand Duke and in my best Russian accent repeated the sentence Vladimir had taught me.

The Grand Duke turned scarlet. Blushing and coughing and at a loss for words, he leaped out of his chair, caught Vladimir by the collar, and soundly boxed his ears.

"How dare you say such a thing to a young lady!" I heard him say as he led Vladimir away.

"But Papa," howled Vladimir, "what is the harm? She didn't know what I was saying!"

It was many years later that I found out what Vladimir had been saying. I knew at the time it was wicked but only later did I discover how naughty it was.

A few years after that incident, the Grand Duke returned to Russia when the czar forgave him for his morganatic marriage and allowed him to resume his rank and estates. But it was an unlucky return. Both the Grand Duke and his wife, as well as my gay little friend, Vladimir, were killed by the Bolshevik revolution.

Celebrities are not always in one generation what they are in the next. Figures of great fame were not always acclaimed by their contemporaries. The same thing also works in reverse.

One of the most famous men of his day was Count Boni de Castellane; today there are few who would recognize his name. If someone were to ask what he was famous for the answer might be confusing. Today, and particularly, I have noticed, in America, the first question usually asked of a man is "What do you do?" The modern world demands that everyone *do* something. There is no room in our society any longer for people who make a career of living.

Count Boni did nothing; by all of today's standards he was a disgrace and a wastrel. Yet in those times and in that society there was a place for a man of charm and elegance, a gentleman of wit and manners. What did he do? He was an asset to any dinner party, a gracious host, and a delightful guest.

Many people have criticized European nobility for marrying wealthy American girls. And yet worse bargains have been made. The count, too, married a rich American, the former Anna Gould. Later she divorced him but even after losing his pink-marble castle and her giant fortune he kept his charm and enchanting sense of humor.

Mme du Bourg de Bozas spent part of each year in Biarritz where she entertained lavishly and often. Usually, I was invited there to spend some weeks. I loved the water and spent much of my time in long walks and lounging on the pale golden sands of Biarritz.

One day the house was filled with a buzz of excitement. Maids scurried about polishing and dusting, flowers were rearranged in vases, and a general uproar was going on as I sauntered in from my day at the beach.

"What is happening?" I asked in surprise.

"Your emperor is coming to dinner," I was told.

My emperor? Who could that be? Knowing little about government I had no idea who my emperor was. I pictured him as an enormous, bejeweled, Oriental potentate—perhaps a cross between my father-in-law, the Maharaja of Kapurthala, and the Dom Pedro of the white satin knee-britches in the portrait.

For the rest of the day until dinner I was in a state of excitement. I could hardly wait to get a look at this magnificent ruler. Although Marie Thérèse and I were not allowed to be present on this important occasion we were permitted to peek from the top of the stairs as the emperor arrived.

As we sat huddled in the damp hall at the top of the landing it seemed forever before the visitor arrived. Marie Thérèse was impatient and teased to go into the playroom. But I begged her to stay and wait with me and hushed her frantically every time her whispering became so loud that I feared being sent away to bed.

Finally, there was much excitement in the downstairs hall. Someone of huge importance was arriving. I leaned over the railing and squinted my eyes to get a better look.

Then, through the front door marched a short, stout, cheerful-looking man dressed in ordinary evening clothes.

Was this my emperor? Crushed with disappointment I turned to Marie Thérèse. She was turning away from the stairs.

"Well, you've seen him," she said impatiently. "Now let's go play."

"But who is that man?" I asked nearly in tears.

"Why, that is your emperor, silly," she said. "That is King Edward VII of England."

I had had no idea that the king of England was also the emperor of India and was bitterly disappointed to discover that an emperor looked like the average Englishman.

The last time I saw King Edward was the following morning on the sands of Biarritz. Yolande and I were frolicking about the beach and chasing a ball thrown by another little girl. As I dashed to catch the ball I tripped and fell flat at the feet of the stout gentleman who was also my emperor.

Terrified by my clumsiness before a king, I leaped to my feet, the sand still clinging to my hair and face. I shuddered to think what emperors did to little girls who behaved in such a fashion. But the emperor of India only smiled, lifted his gray Homburg hat, bowed, and walked on, calling to a small white terrier scampering on the promenade nearby.

Less than a month later the same little terrier trotted in sorrow through the streets of London behind his master's bier. King Edward VII was dead.

Chapter Six

My mother had no idea of the life I was leading so far away from her in France. It was impossible for her to imagine it. For with her incredibly limited experience she could only judge the world by the small glimpses she herself had seen, peering out of the shelter of Indian purdah.

Sometimes after hurrying home from school with Beatrix, both of us giggling and teasing as we rushed to our rooms to change into pretty frocks for a gay evening, I would see on my bureau a letter from my mother. The sight of her round, careful writing, the letters drawn with love and patience, often brought tears to my eyes. I loved my mother and missed her with a yearning I tried to stifle with carelessness and indifference, but when her letters came I could not hide the loneliness that would sweep over my heart.

The peace and quietness in her letters were always a comfort to me. How much like a child she had become to me as I pictured her sitting in the silence of her room, her dark head bent over the letter, laboriously trying to write a mother's devotion into a few lines. She had no words of advice to give me. She could not tell me how to flirt with a boy at a dance or how to wear my hair—she would have been shocked to know that I lived in a world where such things were important. All she could give me was her love and the words of the only guide she knew to life—the Gita. In every letter she reminded me of the Hindu faith in which I had been raised and the duty I owed to my family and country and always quoted a passage from the Gita or a Hindu philosopher. The words brought great comfort to me but sometimes as I read them I thought rebelliously that my mother knew nothing of the world I had been thrust into. It is easy for her, I thought, to give up the world. She has no choice nor has she seen enough of its splendor to want it. But at almost sixteen, the freedom and fun and gaiety were not so easy for me to relinquish.

Wilful and spoiled and sure of my own importance, it was neither so easy to become pure in heart and giving of love as my religion taught me. "Resign everything unto God," wrote my mother. "Seek no praise, no reward, for anything you do. No sooner do we perform a good action than we begin to desire credit for it. Misery must come as the result of such desires." And yet I could not accept her wisdom then. I wanted praise at all times. If I helped Beatrix with anything I expected enormous gratitude; if I performed my studies well I wanted to be applauded. In my heart I did not accept my mother's philosophy of loving with no return. I expected adulation for my very existence.

And yet I was torn by conflict. My early teachings had been of goodness and purity of the soul; yet the world in her flimsy trappings had beckoned to me with an evil finger. I did not want to but I liked that world better than the teachings of my mother.

Her simplicity made her seem like a child. I could not lean on her or tell her about my problems. I felt I had to protect her. Although I was still a young girl, I had become the mother and she was my small, gentle child who was too fragile to face the harsh reality into which I had been plunged. I was beginning to know the terms on which life is lived for most people, the competitive struggle, the jealousies and rages of humanity. I was finding out that a jungle is safer than a tea party and I was determined to protect my mother from such knowledge. So my letters answered her tenderness with insincerity and evasion. It was the only way I knew to return her love.

It was over five years since I had seen my mother and the more I tried to remember the contours of her face, the more shadowy outlines grew dim and receded from me. The faces of the people you love most dearly are almost always the most difficult to recall in their absence. The face of a casual acquaintance can be brought to mind more quickly than that of a lover.

I longed to see my mother again. Her letters had begun to grow shorter and they seemed confused and difficult to read. I thought sadly that it was because we had been separated for such a long time and that now we had grown so far apart that letters could no longer bridge the gap between us.

Then one day Countess Pracomtal brought a letter to me from my father which he had addressed to her.

"My dear child," she said gently, holding my hands in hers, "you must be brave when you read this letter."

My heart twisted inside of me as she handed me the letter. I knew, with an enormous pain, the first terrible anxiety of my life, and childlike did not want to know the news that the message contained. If I could just hand it back and not read it, I thought, perhaps some magic will make the bad news go away. But I knew there was no magic and I had to read the letter.

My mother was dangerously ill, wrote my father, and wanted to see me at once. Even though I had known in my heart that the letter contained bad news of my mother, the shock of the actual words drove me frantic with terror and grief.

"I must go home at once," I cried. "I must see my mother. I know she is dying."

The countess tried to comfort me but I was beyond comfort. I could only picture my mother dying at every moment that I was away from her. As I combed my hair or walked down the street or ate my dinner I wept with fear. All I could think was that at that moment my mother was strangling with death and that I could walk in the sunshine and not know at which moment her eyes closed forever.

The pain of it was more than I could bear. I was desperate to return to India at once. But it was no simple matter. The countess did not have the authority to send me on the long, six-week trip without the express permission of my guardian, the Maharaja of Kapurthala. Weeping with helplessness and sorrow, I begged the countess to intercede with the maharaja to send me home at once. Every moment seemed a dangerous waste of time. I could scarcely live from minute to minute without the paralyzing fear that I would never see my mother alive again.

The countess cabled the maharaja several times but the permission did not come and I could not start on my way without it. Instead, some days later, after an agony of suspense and long endless sleepless nights when I imagined the pains and the dying agonies of my mother, a long cable came from the Maharaja of Kapurthala.

The illness was much exaggerated, he said, there was no real danger, and every prospect indicated that she would recover completely. A miracle, I thought, when the countess read me the cable! How close to nearly lose the one you love most dearly and have her snatched back to you at the last moment. I was even more reassured when her letters began to arrive once again. They were short but cheerful and each one was like a gift from God.

In a month or so all my fears had vanished. Her letters arrived with regularity and I answered each one long and lovingly. Then, early one morning I was handed a cablegram from India. It was from my father and he told me that my mother had died.

I went nearly out of my mind with pain and anguish. I read the cablegram over again and the words were crazy and black against my eyes. I started toward the stairs as

Beatrix came toward me, and twisted over into a heap on the bed. As I fainted my last thoughts were a prayer that I would never wake again to a world so full of cruelty.

All night long I screamed and wept. Not to have seen my mother before she died, the agony of it was too much to bear. What is it one thinks to have by a last look at a loved one but the pain of knowing at that moment they are slipping away? And yet the torment and guilt of not sharing her last moment and not seeing the final look of love alive in her face and to have been happy with lungs full of air as she struggled for breath or to have walked in the Paris sunshine as the darkness closed about her eyes forever was a nightmare that haunted me for years after her death. Over and over after that last awful day I dreamed that I was with her at her death, suffered with her every pain and anguish, and tried to make up for being alive as she was dying.

I could not even go to the funeral since the boat trip would bring me to India long after it was over. All I could do was mourn and weep with sorrow, as I imagined the long and solemn rites taking place. In my grief I decided to observe both the French and Hindu customs of mourning. I would wear black for two years, as they did in France, and give up meat for thirteen days, as is the custom in India. I knew grief was of the heart and that outward manifestations of mourning did not show what I really felt but I wanted to make sure no respect was lacking to the memory of my mother.

My father was half-crazy with shock. He wrote to me

constantly, wailing his sorrow through the many miles that separated us and at last I heard the details of my mother's death.

When my father wrote me for the first time he had just learned that my mother was suffering from cancer and that the disease would be fatal. In the weeks that passed from that time she had sickened and weakened quickly. There was no hope for her and in spite of the fact that my father and the doctors tried to cheer her up by telling her she would soon be well, she knew that her life was at its end.

She talked about dying constantly to my father and worried about her children and what would happen to them after her death, especially the youngest, a girl who was born only a few months before her death.

Near the end, although she hardly had the breath to live through each day, she insisted that she must make a trip to the holy Ganges River to purify herself before death. She was a religious woman and did not want to die before she had performed the rite so important to Hindus of great faith.

The doctor was horrified at this suggestion. He told my father that such a trip would kill my mother but gentle, mild little woman that she was, she insisted that she would go to the Ganges. It was a sad trip, for both my parents knew that it was their last together. But she dressed herself and started on the long twenty-four-hour trip from Simla to the sacred river. She was in unbearable pain and only through enormous control and will was she able to struggle through the hours to reach the Ganges.

She became weaker and weaker and the pain was beginning to consume her. They reached the Ganges just before dawn and could see the white-robed pilgrims meditating along the banks.

"Lift me up so that I can see the river," my mother whispered to my father.

He wiped the perspiration from her head and held her in his arms against the window of the train.

"I can see it," she murmured. "I have reached my goal."

Her lips moved in the traditional Hindu prayer but she was so weak that my father could hear nothing. Then she twisted once in his arms and fell back and died as the train moved closer to the station.

The letter from my father brought me some comfort. I knew my mother had died in peace and in the way she had wanted. But I missed her more than ever and read and reread every letter she had ever written me.

My future father-in-law wrote me a long letter of sympathy and ordered a small, but beautiful, pearl necklace from Cartier as a gift for my sorrow. But I resented the fact that he had kept me from my mother's side and put the necklace away in my drawer. I did not wear it for many years.

The kind countess decided that it would be a good idea for me to leave Paris at this time. I was trying to struggle through the days but was suffering from depression and apathy. I took no interest in anything and moved about only because it was necessary to go from one activity to another. Since it was July the countess planned a trip for all of us to go to Switzerland. We went to the lovely Lake Lucerne where even in summer the snow-capped mountains tower above the blue lakes. Yolande, Beatrix, and I rowed and climbed and sat on the fresh grass on the sides of the Alps.

The gentle air of Switzerland and the change of scene helped me to recover. I began to accept the death of my mother and the inevitability of life. I was beginning to grow up in spite of myself.

But now new thoughts began to crowd into my mind. I could no longer avoid the reality of my own life. Up to that point I had thought little about my future. My engagement to the Tika Raja had been so much a part of my childhood that I had accepted it without question. In France when my young friends asked about my marriage I laughed and tossed it off.

"I am much too young to think about that," I would say.

But I was no longer too young.

The time was coming closer when I must leave France and the life I had learned to love, and return to my duties in India. I remembered the words of my mother. "The word of a Rajput, once given, must be kept." There was no chance of not returning to become the bride of the Tika Raja.

Calamity never strikes singly. Always more than one blow seems to follow closely. So it was with me. The death of my mother had shaken me completely, but the second tragedy nearly destroyed my entire life.

To a European such an event was far from tragic. But to me it was a hopeless burden. I fell in love for the first time with a young French boy.

It was bound to happen. An impressionable young girl caught in the romantic atmosphere of that time would almost certainly find her first love among the young people she was growing up with.

I had known him for some time as a friend of the Pracomtals. His name was not Guy but I shall call him that because even today there are a few friends who knew how much we cared for each other those many years ago.

First love is much the same for everyone, and I, too, was convinced that only a miracle had crossed our lives together. Guy told me about the lovely French fable which says that before two people are born their soul is split in heaven and one part goes to a man and the other half to a woman. If the two souls find each other on earth they have perfect happiness together but if they do not, all through their lives they must search in order to assuage the empty loneliness which comes from being incomplete.

We both believed it, as lovers almost always do, and each felt complete and safe for the first time in our lives. My aching loneliness was replaced by the magic of a dream, of gazing in wonder at the face of my beloved with astonishment that love like that could have happened to me.

Guy was an officer in the army but I saw him at balls and parties when he was home on leave. One evening as we were waltzing together at a ball given by the Comtesse de Fels, he guided me behind a pillar where he told me, as the dancers whirled by us, that he loved me and wanted to marry me.

Until that moment I had thought of Guy only as a

fantasy I could never achieve. After all, I was already engaged and, more important, it never occurred to me that he would be interested in me.

I turned pale as he told me of his love. "You can't mean it," I whispered. "It's too impossible."

He looked at me with his blue eyes which shone like the sea and knit his golden eyebrows together.

"I do love you," he said gravely, "and there is nothing I won't give up for you."

"I cannot marry you," I cried. "You know I am already promised to someone else."

With the passion of youth he seized me by the shoulders and nearly shouted aloud in the ballroom.

"If I cannot have you I have no interest in life," he cried.

I tore out of his grasp. "You must let me go," I said, trying to hold back the tears.

Guy started after me as I fled from the ballroom. I hurried over to my guardian and asked to be taken home at once.

"My dear child," she asked in concern when she saw my flushed face, "is something wrong? Are you ill?"

"Yes," I answered, and began to weep. "I am ill and want to leave the ball."

I went home immediately. But all night long I tossed fitfully in my bed. Guy's face spun about me in the dark room. He was everything I had ever dreamed about. Everything about him was infinitely familiar, like a love that was always destined to be a part of me. He was familiar as all the secret dreams of a person are. Finding him had been like finding myself.

Perhaps because it had all been part of the fantasy that the world outside my narrow gates in India held more enchantment than that which I had known, his very strangeness made him dear to me. All my early recollections of men, even physically, had been of dark Eastern masculinity. My fiancé, remote and brooding, was of the world I had always known.

But seeing Guy was like seeing sunshine for the first time. He was filled with laughter and smiles and gaiety. He had no melancholy about him at all. And his blondness made him glitter in my eyes like a magical god who had come from nowhere to find me. He was what my dreams had been all about.

But from the first I was aware that Guy could only be a dream. I was not European enough to give up everything for love—my Indian training would not let me forget about my responsibilities so quickly.

But Guy was not so easily dissuaded. The day following the ball he appeared at the Pracomtals for tea, and the first chance he got to be alone with me in the garden he began to speak.

"If I could," he said, "I would marry you tomorrow. I am prepared for the difficulties."

"Guy, why do you torture yourself like this—and me? It is impossible. I can never marry you."

"When people love each other," he answered me, walking up and down the garden path, "there must be a way for them."

Women are always somewhat wiser and sadder than men and although I was years younger than Guy, I knew even then that it is not possible to have always what you want out of life.

"Even if I were not engaged," I said, "you forget about the great differences between us."

"There is no difference," Guy answered angrily, "between two people in love."

"What about your family?" I asked. "Europeans have such prejudices. It is one thing for them to accept me socially; it is another to allow their only son to marry me."

Guy turned red with anger. "I can't let you speak that way," he shouted. "Who are we Europeans? What do we mean compared to a culture as old and fine as India?"

"It is useless to argue," I answered sadly. "That's the way the world is. We alone cannot expect it to change for us."

"I cannot let you go," he cried. "It is too much to ask."

"You have very little choice," I said. "You forget that I have my duty and I must return to India."

But it was easier to answer Guy rationally than to answer the terrible pain in my heart. How could I leave him when I loved him so? If I could marry Guy, I thought, life would be as I had always wanted it since coming to Europe. Nothing would change very much. I understood the ways of Europeans by then more than I could believe in my Indian background. I was too rebellious for India, too defiant to go back to a life where I would remain half-veiled physically and emotionally. There was no submission in me.

In the months that followed our declaration of love we

tortured each other with terrible scenes. The agony was heightened by the fact that we could never be really alone. We saw each other frequently since we were constantly at the same parties and receptions, but in those days a solitary rendezvous was impossible. So we snatched moments alone at parties and balls but never had but a few minutes before some interruption came to separate us.

Leaving out my own responsibilities, my judgment was quite correct about Guy's family. They were ardent Catholics and the marriage of their son to a Hindu, which they considered a heathen religion, was unthinkable. I realized that I was alone in France. I was a Hindu and despite the kindness and welcome shown to me in Europe, there was a vast difference between the two worlds. It was not expected that I would attempt to bridge it.

Guy wanted me to elope. "We'll go to the register's office," he said. "And once it's done they'll just have to accept it."

For days I was torn with indecision. Suddenly the thought of returning to India to marry a man I did not know or understand was unbearable. And the time was galloping toward me when I would have to leave on the long journey across the black sea.

Guy even went to his grandmother, a kind, dear old lady who knew and loved me. She told him she would help him and give him the money to marry me.

So, it could be possible after all. The real barrier left was me. I was sick with conflict. I could not eat or sleep and each time the doorbell rang I jumped with nervousness. I had to talk to someone. But there was no one to talk to.

Finally one night Yolande came to me. "Everyone is talking about you," she said.

My heart leaped in terror. Then they all knew already the dreadful secret of our love.

"You look so ill," she said. "They want to know what's the matter with you. Can't you tell me?"

I sank back on the bed in relief. Then I began to sob with exhaustion and all the pent-up emotions I had kept inside for so many months. I decided to tell Yolande everything.

Yolande's viewpoint was harsh but practical.

"There is no future in such a romance," she said. "Give him up at once and forget about him. You could not be happy together if all around you, you had created misery."

I knew that what she said was true and was determined to follow her advice. The following day I saw Guy and told him that we must forget each other. A most dreadful scene followed with both of us weeping and torn apart with the agony of separation. But when we parted nothing had been settled. We were too much in love to be strong.

That night in my pain I did something I had never done before. I prayed, not to the gods of Hinduism but to the Holy Virgin of the Christians, holding in my hands the picture which Comtesse d'Eu had given me years before.

I woke hours later after a dream. My mother, looking as she had the last time I bid her good-by, had come to me and said, "A Rajput cannot go back on her word. You must be married as you promised. This man is an untouchable; if you marry him you will be a woman without country or race and all your family will share your disgrace."

Perhaps it was my own conscience talking. But it filled me with a determination and resolve I had been incapable of before. The next day I told Guy of my dream and he knew finally that there was no longer any hope.

But I could not stop loving him. He was often in my thoughts. And when he was killed in the war in 1916 I grieved his death and could not believe that this young blond giant of my dreams was no more. I have mourned him ever since.

Chapter Seven

It was time to put aside my own desires and return to India. I was sixteen and my European education was over; now I had to do what was expected of me. I told myself sternly that I must put Guy out of my mind but it was not easy. In the weeks that followed I was determined to be brave and dutiful, yet it seemed to me that I would never wake again and be glad to see the sunshine. Is there a greater desolation than that which follows loss of love when you are young enough to believe that life brings happiness? At the time I did not think so.

My marriage was destined from the start to make history in many ways. For one thing, it was the first time since the Kapurthala house had gone to the Sikh faith that they were marrying back into the Rajput dynasty. It was also the first princely wedding ceremony in India to be held in public and the first to be filmed by the newsreels.

The maharajah insisted that I purchase an elaborate trousseau and in the few remaining weeks before returning to India, Mme de Pracomtal and I feverishly shopped in Paris. My future father-in-law had presented me with a blank check to cover all the expenses, and my wardrobe was lavish. Even my lingerie was handmade, marked with my monogram, and trimmed with fragile Valenciennes lace. I was too young not to have had some pleasure from the luxury of pretty things and the purchases kept me from thinking too much about all I would soon be leaving behind.

I said good-by to my friends one gray December day as rain sleeted on the streets of Paris. I couldn't help weeping when I parted with Beatrix and Yolande Pracomtal. They had become more like sisters to me than my own.

Mme de Pracomtal was taking me to India by boat. I was grateful that I did not have to make the trip alone because I was filled with fear and apprehension at the thought of my return. Luckily, one of my young friends, Arlette de Failly, was also making the trip to India at the same time, as well as my future brothers-in-law, Princes Amarjat and Mahajit. The long trip was strange and exciting and we behaved like carefree children. For the weeks on the dark waters I forgot the real purpose of my return to India.

It was strange to be back in India. In Bombay I felt like a foreigner; the noises and smells were so different from France. Even my own countrymen looked like people from another world.

After spending several days in Bombay with the countess showing us the sights—just as though I had never set foot in India before—we left by train for Kapurthala. On our arrival there Arlette and her mother went to the guest house, the two princes to the main palace, and I to the women's palace. I traveled from the railway station to the palace in a closed carriage; for the first time in many years I was back in purdah.

I was met at the women's palace by the maharaja's three wives. They greeted me with kindness and chattered with delight over my appearance. But they only woke in me a desperate loneliness for my own mother. How happy she would have been to see me, how tenderly she would have embraced her child again. And I needed her that moment more than ever. If only there had been someone to give me a few words of comfort and reassurance. Someone to tell me that everything was going to be all right, that by doing my duty, my desperation and hopelessness would leave me. But there was no one.

As soon as I could make my excuses, I hurried away to my rooms. There I found my cheerful, rosy-cheeked Italian maid who had been with me in France. The sight of her bustling about unpacking my clothes as if no tragedy were about to take place made me feel less forlorn. I sat watching her for awhile as she went about her work efficiently and couldn't help giggling at the two Indian ayahs who ran about the room, accomplishing nothing except salaaming to me in unison, touching first the ground and then their foreheads with their curved palms, babbling all the while in what sounded like a queer and foreign tongue.

At last I dried my tears, bathed, and changed into Indian clothes. I looked into the mirror for a long time. It seemed strange to believe that from now on I was to be the girl who looked back soberly in a shimmering sari. As I turned from the mirror there was a knock on the door. My little maid ran to answer it and my father, brothers, and sisters walked in.

At first I did not know them. In five years they had all changed so much. My brothers and sisters were just as bewildered to see me and for the first half hour of our time together we sat in embarrassment hardly able to say a word. Gradually, however, I began to speak and then my brothers and sisters joined in. My father, however, was so overcome with emotion that tears came to his eyes as he tried to talk. I, too, was moved by my home-coming and all of us ended up weeping in each other's arms.

The wedding day was planned for three weeks from the day of my arrival. This date was no haphazard choice but one carefully determined long in advance by the astrologers. There was a good time for such occasions and a bad time. It was necessary that a princess be married on the most auspicious date possible.

I was kept busy every moment in the next few weeks. I had to relearn my language and remember the old customs which had slipped from my mind in my years abroad. I was neither happy nor unhappy. In the excitement of the preparations there was little time for meditation.

The wedding plans were on a giant scale. In all Indian states the marriage of the heir is an occasion of enormous importance and my future father-in-law loved pomp and excitement. Guests began to arrive in scores from all over the country; several dozen rulers sent their eldest sons while nine of them attended in person.

One of the principal guests was the Maharaja of Kashmir

and Jammu whose previous rulers had declared themselves blood brothers with Kapurthala in a special ceremony. Aga Khan, although not a ruler in the territorial sense, was the chief Moslem guest.

Since my father-in-law loved foreign travel, he had hundreds of friends all over the world. For these guests he arranged a special date for a steamer to sail from Marseille to bring them to India. At least a hundred came from France and about three hundred from England and North and South America. Many of my old friends arrived and I was delighted to see them again. For the moment India did not seem far away from Europe.

In the weeks before my wedding I tried not to think too much about my own personal future and what marriage would mean to me. Romantically, my thoughts were still with Guy and, although I was determined never to see him again, it was impossible to consider someone else in the same way. So I concentrated on the mounting excitement of the coming ceremony and the festivities which surrounded it. I pushed out of my mind that there would be another person connected with my marriage.

A festivity in India brings not only invited guests but hordes of sight-seers. From all over the country hundreds and thousands of beggars, holy men, would-be workers of miracles, and promoters of fertility began to arrive. They flocked into Kapurthala by train, on foot, by cart, and on every sort of beast. Nor were they unwelcome, for tradition decreed that they were every bit as important as the princes invited by His Highness. In fact, the host of such a wedding was expected to provide fireworks and lavish feasts for the beggars who crowded around the grounds of the palace.

Two days before my wedding, the maharaja held an enormous public reception, called a *grand durbar,* to welcome his guests. Here the officials of the state presented their congratulations and gifts, and the wedding festivities began. I saw nothing of any of these. There were to be no feasts for me. That was part of my life in France. In India I was expected to remain docilely in purdah. I rebelled a little at the sounds of gaiety I could hear through the walls of the palace but I tried to reconcile myself to my new life.

The maharaja brought a dance orchestra from Bombay and gave a huge ball for his European guests. Before the ball there was an elaborate Western banquet at which eight hundred guests were served, and while they ate and drank, cannon were fired outside the palace walls. The following night, on the eve of my wedding, a lavish Oriental feast was prepared for even more guests who celebrated most of the night.

I was wakened on my wedding day by my Italian maid. Dawn was breaking and the stark room was faintly touched by the color of the sky. I opened my eyes drowsily and yawned. The noise of the fireworks and shouting of the guests had made my sleep restless. I was still tired.

Exasperated by my laziness, my maid chattered at me in Italian and shook my shoulders.

"You cannot be late on your wedding day," she said reprovingly. "It is time to get up."

As with Mlle Meillon, I tried to sneak a few more

minutes of precious sleep. It was always easier for me to put something off. I pulled the covers over my head and buried my face in the pillows. I could hear Maria's despairing sighs as she tried to rouse me.

"I'll get up soon," I assured her in a muffled voice. But I knew I would sleep until the last moment. As I tried to go back to sleep I realized I was no longer a schoolgirl. I could not expect others to force me to accept my responsibilities. It was time for me to do what I had to do because of my own knowledge of what was right. I sat up in bed sleepily.

"You are perfectly right, Maria," I said. "I should have been up long ago."

During the night my sleep had been fitful, not only because of the noises around me but also because I began to dread a marriage which now seemed, after my years in Europe, to be primitive and without feeling. How could a man and woman marry without love? I had tossed and fretted most of the night pondering that question.

But as the dawn began to glow in the room, I became reconciled. It was my fate to be a princess and to marry the heir of an important state. I loved glitter and excitement; perhaps that would be what my life was going to be like.

After I bathed, Maria, my Indian ayahs, and the wives of the maharaja helped me into my wedding dress. I gasped with delight when I saw it. It was like wearing a gossamer rainbow with the sun sparkling through it.

In India, white is for poor women and widows—the traditional wedding gown for others must be dazzling in its brilliance. I did not wear a sari but wore the national dress style of my state, called *eholu* in my hill dialect, a dress with long tight sleeves, a fitted bodice, and full skirt over tight trousers which were gathered about my ankles.

My dress, which took two years to weave by hand, was of a fragile, chiffon-like material woven of red silk and strands of pure gold. On my head floated a veil of gold cloth which flashed with many colors of silken threads. About my throat was twisted strands of creamy pearls—part of the treasure of the state of Kapurthala. My feet, which had been bathed and anointed with precious creams, were placed into delicate sandals and about my ankles jeweled bracelets studded with diamonds, rubies, and emeralds were fastened. On one toe I wore a large, ornately carved, gold ring.

Each step in my dressing was part of the ceremony. Prayers were said over me as I dressed my hair, an elaborate process that took nearly two hours. By the time I was completely dressed, I was already fatigued. But the long wedding day had just begun.

In another part of the palace, my husband-to-be, the Tika Raja, was beginning his part of the ceremony. Although I did not see any of his preparations, I was told about it later by my sisters and saw such a ceremony for myself many times later when friends and relatives married in similar ceremonies.

In the main courtyard, thousands of women were gathered to watch these ceremonial preparations. The only males allowed here were the Tika Raja and the Brahmin priests who led him into the center of the court. After the sacred fire was lit the chanting of the women and priests began.

For this ceremony the Tika Raja wore a loose white *dhoti*, a Hindu garment which begins at the waist and hangs in folds about the legs to just above the ankles.

After the fire-worship was over, the traditional bathing and anointing of the bridegroom began. His mother, his aunt, and a female relative set to work, rubbing and scrubbing him with mounds of suds made from Indian soaps and perfumed waters. All the women in the courtyard laughed and shrieked as he shouted for mercy from the scrubbings. (This ceremony is one time when the women of India have the upper hand and they enjoy it to the utmost.)

Then the Tika Raja re-entered the palace, bathed and anointed until he shone. Not long afterward the Tika Raja strode out wearing the ceremonial dress of his state, a garment which was centuries old in its style. The coat was of shining scarlet silk with thousands of perfect pearls sewn on it in the design of flowers, caught to the jacket with gold silk and crimson thread. The jacket was tight about his waist and arms, flaring out to well below his knees.

He wore a small turban on his head. A glittering pin of diamonds and emeralds fastened feathers to the turban and he carried a sword in a scabbard completely covered with precious stones. More rubies and diamonds flashed at his throat, in his ears, and on his fingers. Even his slippers of gold thread were interlaced with jewels. For the first moment when I saw him, I could not believe he was real; the sun shining on his jewels and brilliant costume made him look like a legendary prince out of the *Arabian Nights.*

At eight o'clock in the morning my preparations were over and whispering a short prayer in Hindu (and one in French when no one was listening) I left the small palace where I had dressed and set out for the large courtyard of the main palace where the wedding ceremony was to take place.

Trembling with excitement, I stared at the large elephant who had come to take me away. Way up, nearly up to the sky it seemed to me, on the elephant's back, was a howdah, made like a jeweled throne, in which I was to sit. My jewels and veils were adjusted, the last-minute chattering and mumbled prayers were said over me, and the heavy silken curtains of the howdah were drawn together to conceal me from the thousands of people gathered about.

The elephant moved slowly through the grounds of the palace. By this time I was too numb with excitement to think but I sat in the close, musty howdah with my hands folded and my lips trembling. I could see nothing, but the noise outside the curtains was deafening. The shouts and screams, chanting of prayers, and the footsteps of thousands of people sounded like thunder in my ears.

At last the slow, rocking motion of the elephant stopped. We had reached the entrance to the grand courtyard. I felt the huge beast sink slowly to his knees, then the silken curtains of the howdah parted and the blazing sun rushed in to blind me after the darkness.

My father, with the high priest who was gowned in spotless white, reached out his hand and helped me down from the elephant. Together we walked slowly up a narrow carpet strewn with flowers which led to an altar erected at the same end of the enormous courtyard. All about me thousands of faces stared but seemed only a blur of color. I was too shy to look at anyone but kept my eyes straight ahead.

The ceremony itself was six hours long. Part of the time was spent in long chants by priests in order to pacify the planets so that my husband and I would have a long and happy life and be blessed by heirs. Bored and tired by the long chanting, I stole many looks at my future husband who sat beside me. He, too, looked bored and unhappy but we did not catch each other's eyes or smile.

The Maharaja of Kapurthala was a blazing figure that day. Dressed in a suit of gold brocade with his throat, chest, and wrists sparkling with diamonds and pearls, my father-in-law was triumphant on the day of my marriage. Beneath his gleaming gold turban, crowned with an emerald tiara, his dark eyes flashed with the satisfaction of a leader who brought his house back into the dynasty of Rajput.

His Highness was determined that his son's wedding go down in Indian history. Custom decrees that the bride and groom leave the wedding separately, the woman discreetly veiled and curtained. Instead, the Tika Raja and I drove side by side in an open state carriage with the deafening din of the crowds resounding in our ears.

For my father-in-law, it was a bold blow at purdah and one which excited a considerable comment in the state.

Afterward he continued to defy convention; he never asked me to resume purdah again except when the more orthodox women of the family were present.

Escorted by a troop of bodyguards we drove through the streets of Kapurthala. When our drive was over we attended two receptions, one at the women's palace where we greeted hundreds of Indian women guests, the other at the main palace where Europeans and Indian males feasted and celebrated our marriage.

By nightfall I was exhausted from the celebrations. I yearned to escape to the cool solitude of my rooms and be soothed and bathed by my little maid but instead the Tika Raja and I were driven to a small house on the palace grounds where we were to spend the next few days before starting on our honeymoon.

The servants greeted us at the door, tended to our wants, then bowed and departed. The Tika Raja and I were alone.

He sat in one corner of the room on a low cushion; I was at the other end of the room. Neither of us spoke. The Tika Raja stared at me.

My heart was pounding with the tension and fatigue of the day. For the first time I realized that we were to be alone together for the rest of our lives. And I was overwhelmed by the thought that my husband was a complete stranger to me.

I moved restlessly on the cushion. I wanted desperately to escape or to break the trembling silence. Yet I did not know what to do or what to say.

I pretended to yawn. The Tika Raja still stared but did not appear to notice my yawning. I moved about self-consciously under his gaze. Why doesn't he speak, I thought.

The room grew heavy with tension. My head felt light and weak from the strain, not only of the moment but of the days and weeks which had preceded it. I could not bear it another moment.

"I'm very tired," I whispered, my voice hoarse and indistinct from embarrassment. I half rose from the cushion.

The Tika Raja got up and walked toward me. He stood over me and looked down at me, his dark eyes burning. His face looked strange and different from the way I had remembered it. The sulkiness was gone, replaced by a tense, fiery expression. This time it was my turn to stare. The boy I had known was gone and a man returned my gaze though I was certain that inwardly he too was shy.

He reached down for my hands and helped me to my feet. Numbly I rose and allowed him to lead me from the room.

He showed me into another room. I saw with relief that it was a bedroom. I was tired and worn out. I could hardly wait for sleep to overtake me.

"This is our room," he said.

"*Our* room?" I repeated in disbelief.

"Why, yes, of course," he answered. "What did you expect?"

"Why, naturally, I expected my own room," I said in a muffled voice.

"But you are married now," he replied.

Suddenly I was filled with terror. What did he mean by this?

"That makes no difference to me," I cried. "I have never

slept in the same room with anyone and I cannot begin it now."

The Tika Raja's face grew stern and his mouth tightened.

"You don't know what you are saying," he said.

"Oh, yes, I do," I cried defiantly, now close to panic. "I want to go to my own room."

He took a step toward me, then stopped abruptly.

Now it was all too much for me. The fatigue and tensions of the past months, the exhaustion and fears of my wedding day overcame me. I leaned against the door of my bedroom and burying my face in my hands like a little girl, sobbed and sobbed, the hot tears spilling down my cheeks and onto my dress.

The Tika Raja put his hands on my shoulders gently. Then he lifted my face up to his and looked in it long and searchingly. His face was different once again. The manliness was still there but the sternness had been replaced with tenderness.

"My dear child," he said in a soft, wondering voice. "Did no one tell you what marriage would be like?"

I shook my head dumbly, wishing then that someone had told me what marriage meant.

"What did you think it would be like to be married?" he asked me.

I dried my tears on the sleeve of my dress. "I don't know," I answered in a small voice. "I didn't think anything would be different at all. Why does it have to be different?" I asked.

The Tika Raja drew me to a low mat on the floor and

sat down beside me. He stroked my hair and began to speak. In a voice full of kindness he told me that he loved me and explained that we were now husband and wife. Gently he told me what marriage meant.

I listened attentively. Because of his kindness my terror ebbed away. I was infinitely comforted by his gentleness. I realized as he spoke that although I was only sixteen, I was a woman now and had to accept all the responsibilities of my marriage.

Then the Tika Raja, in a sweet, awkward attempt to comfort me, told me about our honeymoon plans and the life we would lead on our return. Like the child I was, my spirits rose when I heard the happy plans for our future.

I smiled hopefully, the tears dry now on my face, when I learned we would visit the Taj Mahal, and was even more delighted when my husband told me that my beloved Countess de Pracomtal would accompany us on our trip.

I clapped my hands with happiness. "It will be much more fun," I said in delight, "with three of us on our honeymoon!"

Young as he was, the Tika Raja had to smile with amusement. I smiled back. It seemed then that everything was going to be all right.

But as I look back now after so many years I realize there was no way for my wedding night to be a happy one. I was still only a child. Even his gentleness could not make up for my innocence.

Chapter Eight

Few things in life come up to one's expectations but the sight of the Taj Mahal left me breathless. The first time we saw it was in the moonlight, with the pale moon shimmering over the marble. As we stood watching, I shuddered, remembering the beautiful young princess in whose memory the Taj had been erected. In the midst of the night I could feel her haunting spirit quiver above the pool of silver.

But I was even more delighted with the Taj Mahal at dawn. I have always loved the moment when the first light explodes in the sky; to me it is a constant miracle to watch the blackness part to let the sun come through. But both the Tika Raja and the countess tried to dissuade me from visiting the Taj Mahal at dawn. My husband and I had our first quarrel about it.

"I'm not interested in seeing it again," he said crossly.

"We have already seen it once, my dear," said the countess.

"If you don't want to see it you don't have to," I answered. "I shall go alone."

"Alone!" shouted the Tika Raja. "What are you thinking of? This is not France where you can go about alone!"

"I can take care of myself," I said.

"You must put all those ideas out of your head at once," my husband answered. "You are my wife now and must do as I say."

I glared at my husband. "And if I refuse?"

The Tika Raja's face grew stern. He banged his fist down on the table, then stood up. His voice was icy.

"There is no such thing as refusal," he said coldly. "It is up to you to obey me and I say you cannot go anywhere alone!"

I started to answer him but the countess put a friendly hand on my shoulder.

"My child," she said gently, "the Tika Raja is right. You are his wife and it is your duty to obey him."

I tried to fight back the tears. I would not let him see that he had made me cry, but I was vastly humiliated. How dare he say that I must obey him? Was this what marriage was like? Where was the tenderness he had showed me on our wedding day? Had it ended forever? I wanted understanding and love. And I was too spoiled to accept anything else.

But the countess was wiser than either of us. She knew the quarrels of youth and inexperience and knew also the value of compromise.

"I shall accompany you to the Taj Mahal at dawn," she said. "Perhaps it is a good idea, after all."

In the end the Tika Raja came with us. He could not bear to be left out of anything and rather than stay home and sulk he came along. After we were there he acted as if seeing the Taj Mahal at dawn had been his idea entirely. It took me days to forgive what I considered his unreasonable attitude for I did not know then that all men have much in common in such things.

I was also worried because I knew in my heart he was right. As the wife of an Indian prince I was expected to obey his wishes. But I knew my defiant and rebellious nature and wondered whether I could ever learn to submit. Where would my wilfulness lead me, I thought with a pang of fear.

We were all glad that we had seen the Taj Mahal in the dawn. The sky, painted with pink and gold, touched the marble with flecks of color so that the Taj seemed to come alive and the color glowed as if the monument were lighted from within. I gasped at the beauty of it and whispered a good-by to the princess whose spirit in the dawn must surely have been a happy one.

Before arriving in Agra, we had spent some time in Delhi where we behaved like tourists who had never seen India before, wandering about the city, visiting the points of interest. Countess de Pracomtal was shocked by this intimate view of India. All the Indians the countess had known were elegant, educated, well-traveled people she had met in Paris. Now for the first time she was seeing the real India, the India of filth and poverty, the India of vastness and ignorance. It was far different from anything she had seen before.

I, too, was shocked by much of what I saw. In spite of the fact that I had traveled much for a girl of sixteen, it had been the most sheltered and isolated sort of existence. Always I stayed at elegant hotels and was kept at a distance from the poverty of slums. In my years in Paris I had avoided the poor sections of the city. But in Delhi and other parts of India where we were now traveling, it was impossible to escape the sight of poverty. The overwhelming population of India is something one cannot avoid. The millions of hungry faces and naked children living in dirt and squalor were a shock.

For in spite of my absorption in my own problems, it was on my honeymoon that I became aware of my responsibility to humanity. I was appalled by what I saw and secretly determined that someday I would try to help these wretched people.

We left Agra and my beloved Taj Mahal and went to Bombay. Now it was time for the Countess de Pracomtal to leave us. She was returning to Europe. We said good-by on the hot pier in Bombay and as she turned to go I ran after her and flung my arms around her neck in a good-by embrace. In a way she was the only mother I had known for the last few years and now she was leaving. My heart sank as the boat whistled and made its way slowly out of the harbor. The countess had been a great comfort to me; I was not so sure that I could stand to be on my own.

But my husband was delighted at her departure. Not that he did not like the countess, but he was glad to be alone with me. I also think he felt that two women, no matter how mature and kind the countess was, would naturally be in league with each other. Perhaps he was right.

From Bombay we continued our trip to Baroda where we visited the Maharaja of Baroda and his famous Maharani who was considered one of the most beautiful women of her generation. Compared to the size of Kapurthala and Jubbal, the state of Baroda was gigantic. I was both disappointed and a little amused, however, by the palace at Baroda. Built many years before, it was enormous and ornate, but architecturally it was a combination of every style of European building of its time.

We were entertained lavishly by the maharaja. One of the most exciting, if frightening, spectacles we saw was a wrestling match between elephants. It was an awesome sight to see the two giant animals tumble over on each other and the crowd watching held its breath. I wanted to be polite but I could not watch the elephants fight without being sick; I turned my head away in order not to see them. It was much more fun to watch the tame parrots who fired off miniature cannon and waddled about in a perfect imitation of soldiers.

For the first time I attended a large Indian banquet in Baroda. Before each guest a gold tray was placed which held twelve small bowls, also of gold, filled with curries, meats, and vegetables. Each guest was also given a rice platter and water jug made of gold as well; the fabulously rich maharaja had a complete dinner service in gold to serve one hundred and fifty guests.

It had been a long time since I had had a whole meal in

Indian fashion and I discovered that I had forgotten how to eat it. I couldn't even remember how to handle the *chupati*, or round, wafer pancake which is part of every meal. Blushing with embarrassment as I struggled with the *chupati* with both hands, I tried to watch the rest of the guests to find out how to use it. Finally, the maharaja came to my rescue.

"You are not so much an Indian girl any longer, are you?" he asked, smiling with amusement.

I agreed that my years away from India had made me a stranger in many lands. Awkwardly I tried to imitate the maharaja as he showed me how to hold my *chupati;* with the fourth finger of his right hand he held the pancake flat on the tray, then with thumb and index finger tore off a piece, folded it deftly, and dipped it into the various bowls. In this way each dish is eaten without the aid of a knife, spoon, or fork. Only the right hand is used for eating; the left is reserved for drinking. After the meal was over, the servants hurried in and gave each guest two bowls of water. One bowl was used to rinse the mouth, the other was used as a finger bowl.

During my visit to Baroda the atmosphere there was far from tranquil. Princess Indira, the only daughter of the maharaja, was trying to defy her parents' wishes in regard to a marriage they had arranged for her. At the time she was engaged to the Maharaja of Gwalior, ruler of a nearby state, but she was very upset about the proposed match.

Indira and I became close friends. On my part, I was already lonesome for feminine companionship; I was not accustomed to the isolation of our honeymoon. Indira, too, was grateful for the chance to talk to a girl her own age about her problems. I was full of advice; it is easy to solve other people's problems. But in the end I could only suggest that she follow the same path of action as mine.

"You will be happier, Indira," I said, "if you obey your parents and not defy them."

"But I cannot do it, Brinda," she answered. "Gwalior is an orthodox Hindu who already has a wife. I cannot be a second wife to any man."

"You must put aside your own desires and do what is right. There is no other way."

Indira fell on the bed and buried her face in her hands. "You can't possibly understand, Brinda," she cried. "All my life my father has taught me to think for myself. He has looked on the ignorance and subservience of Indian women with contempt. Now he wants to force me into a marriage that is medieval. How can he do such a thing to me?"

I nodded in agreement. Had not the very same thing happened to me? Perhaps my whole life would have been different if I had remained in India instead of being sent to France. Perhaps I would not have had to rebel against my marriage. Perhaps I would never have known the torture of rejecting a love I really wanted. My heart ached for Indira for I knew too well all that she was feeling. And yet I could see no other solution for her than obedience just as I had been able to see no other way out for myself.

We talked for hours and I tried to show Indira that my course had been the wisest and that at least I had found some peace of mind in acceding to the wishes of my family. But Indira was determined to break off the match. Nothing I said seemed to make any impression on her, and when the

Tika Raja and I left Baroda I was firmly convinced that her marriage to Gwalior would never take place.

I was right. A few months later Indira met the handsome young prince from Cooch-Behar and they fell in love. Armed then with the prospect of real happiness, Indira broke off her engagement to Gwalior. He took it well but her parents were furious. They particularly opposed the engagement on religious grounds since the Cooch-Behars were apostate Hindus, members of the most modern Brahmo-Samaj sect. The orthodox Barodas were aghast at the thought of such a match.

Princess Indira was determined that her marriage to the prince take place, and the young prince was supported in his wishes by his brother, the Maharaja of Cooch-Behar. The young couple attempted to elope but at the last moment Indira was carried off to Europe by her parents. The story of their attempted elopement attracted attention throughout the world and sympathy everywhere was strongly in favor of the thwarted lovers.

After Indira was swept away to Europe her young prince followed on the next boat. Finally in Switzerland, after much pleading, the Maharaja of Baroda reluctantly agreed to the match. A radiant Indira and a happy bridegroom were triumphantly married in a register's office in London. A few months later Prince Jitendra's brother died and Indira and her prince became the Maharaja and Maharani of Cooch-Behar. They had a happy life together but it was many years before Indira healed the breach between herself and her parents.

We left Baroda and returned to Kapurthala. At first, arrangements were made so that the Tika Raja and I would live in the same palace as his father, but I objected. I felt that if we were to be happy at all in our marriage, it was necessary to have as little family interference as possible.

"You must speak to your father," I said firmly, "and tell him that we must have a house of our own."

"What difference does it make?" he asked. "There is plenty of room in the palace."

"But I don't want to live in the palace," I answered. "We are no longer babies. We must have our independence."

Finally I persuaded my husband to speak to his father. Although the Tika Raja was hot-tempered and quick to anger, he had little desire for independence and was perfectly willing to go along, even after his marriage, being treated like a small boy by his father. I, on the other hand, felt that I had made some sacrifices for our marriage and wanted to make a success of it if it was possible. At first the maharaja tried to insist that we remain in the palace but when he saw that we were determined to have our own way, he gracefully gave in and offered us a small but charming house about four miles away from the palace.

The Maharaja of Kapurthala was a stubborn, domineering man who was used to getting his own way in all things. It was somewhat of a surprise to me that he gave in so quickly to our wishes. Later I realized that it was in the nature of a bargain. He was doing it to win my favor. At that time I did not know why.

Soon after we moved into our small house I realized what had been in my father-in-law's mind. He badly needed all the friends he could get to be on his side, for he had just married again for the sixth time and his family and entourage had taken the news very badly.

He had fallen madly in love with a Spanish dancer some months before, while visiting Europe. He married her there and brought her back to the palace at Kapurthala. Then he insisted that she was the princess of the house and expected everyone to treat her as the ranking maharani. Naturally, this was deeply resented by his other wives, who were all Indian women of high caste and orthodox upbringing. Even I was shocked at his unfeeling attitude.

It was on this issue that the maharaja and I first disagreed. Although I was a young girl I could not help criticizing him, at least in my own mind, for his lack of feeling and the fact that he was unable to adhere to what was so clearly his duty. The maharaja was deeply disappointed and angered by my attitude. He considered me a modern woman and resented the fact that my years in Europe had not broadened my attitude to the point where I would accept his rebellion against convention. Perhaps if I had been a little older and a bit more experienced I would have been tolerant. But I felt then that if I, as a young girl, had been able to accept the responsibilities of my marriage and position, that he, as ruler of a state, should have been able to do the same.

My husband, the Tika Raja, was angry for a different reason. The maharaja's affection for my husband's mother, the first maharani, was now shifting to his newly-wed wife. My husband's mother felt bitterly rejected and appealed to my husband to intercede with his father.

Stirred up by his mother and resentful that the maharaja's latest wife had usurped her place, the Tika Raja told his father exactly how he felt. The maharaja was furious at his impertinence and angrily berated his son for daring to criticize his father's affairs.

In the meantime, it was up to me to come to some kind of decision on the matter. I was not exactly free to choose according to my own inclinations. As a princess, raised in the Hindu tradition, I knew that my father-in-law's actions could not be condoned by me, and as a woman, educated in Europe, I could not help but be sympathetic to my husband's mother whose heart was breaking at being cast aside by her husband. I was also sympathetic to the Spanish dancer who was now in the middle of a family quarrel through no fault of her own. The Tika Raja and I discussed the problem many times but in the end there seemed to be only one decision—that we could not countenance this marriage. We refused to meet his wife and stayed away from all royal functions when we knew she would be present. The maharaja never forgave me this decision, for he felt that I was responsible; he always accused me of influencing his son against him.

The beginning of marriage is always a difficult time and we had our own problems in getting along with each other. One of the greatest obstacles to our happiness seemed to be the fact that my husband had nothing to do. We had all the money and material possessions we needed and it was not necessary for him to do anything in exchange for them. He had no interest in politics or in affairs of the state and his father did not force him to take an interest.

As a result he spent his days wandering about our house and the palace grounds. He was restless and moody but even I could see the fault lay with the aimlessness of his existence. Sometimes he would sit for hours staring at a folded newspaper. He seemed depressed and unhappy but when I questioned him he became angry. Often he provoked quarrels with me for no reason. It was almost as though he were so bored that even anger was better than nothing. At least it was something to do.

I felt helpless. I tried to be cheerful but nothing I did seemed to help. Finally, in desperation, I went to the maharaja even though I knew he was still angry with me.

"Perhaps if the Tika Raja had something to do," I began hesitatingly, "he would be happier."

"Do? What is there for him to do?" the maharaja asked sharply.

"Is there no job he could have in the government?"

The maharaja's face grew red. "I am running this state," he said, "and I don't need any help. Let my son amuse himself. What better thing can he do?"

I turned away sadly. If only I could make him understand, I thought, that he was not helping his son by allowing such idleness but only destroying him. But there was nothing more I could do about it for the moment.

As for me, I could not bear the aimlessness of our existence. Up until the time of our marriage, my life had been filled with activity. Now suddenly I had nothing to do with my time.

I thought perhaps I could be of some help to the people of the state. I had been truly shocked and appalled by the poverty I had seen on our honeymoon. Millions of people lay dying and starving in filth and misery. My own mother had tried to help the poor, and I, too, wanted to do all I could. But everywhere I went a door was shut in my face.

My father-in-law was incensed at what he called my interference. He blamed it on my European education and accused me of trying to assert my independence at his expense. Furthermore, he told me that he was not the only one who was displeased with my conduct. Other members of the family, officials of the state, even the servants, had begun to resent me. They criticized the way I dressed my hair, the way I ran my house, my European education—there was nothing about me that someone did not resent. Perhaps it was only natural. In their eyes it must have seemed that I had everything. But young and sensitive, I was made wretched by their hostility.

Crushed by the experience, I asked my husband to take me away to the hills, to Dalhousie, but we were both miserable there. I was exhausted from the strain of the last weeks in Kapurthala and was feeling ill as well. I was glad to return to Kapurthala where we were to accompany the maharaja to the Coronation Durbar in Delhi.

The spectacle of the durbar of King George and Queen Mary was unforgettable. Thousands of Indians acclaimed them in Delhi, shouting their loyalty in the dusty streets. Although I did not meet King George at the time, I accompanied my husband's mother to a purdah garden party given in honor of the queen.

The maharani knew little English but by that time I had acquired quite a bit of knowledge of the language although I spoke it with a French accent. When we were presented to the queen, Her Majesty greeted us graciously, addressing to my mother-in-law a few simple remarks, in English, which she had no difficulty in understanding. The maharani struggled to answer with one or two carefully rehearsed English sentences which she carried off very well.

Then Queen Mary turned to me and spoke in perfect French. I was so astonished that every word of French fled from my head and I answered her, stammering in English, "Yes, Your Majesty!"

"Why, you speak English, too—how clever of you!" answered the Queen. "I was told you spoke none at all, only French."

I still could not answer in French but at least was able to remember enough English to say, "Yes, Your Majesty, I am learning English now."

With relief I saw that the next guest was about to be presented and the maharani and I retired. But I left the party impressed most of all with the graciousness of the queen who I have been told suffered all her life from acute shyness which she overcame only by the greatest self-control. Even then I appreciated her kindness and thoughtfulness in remembering to speak French to me in order to put me at my ease—it was certainly not her fault that my memory had become a blank.

Back in Kapurthala the reason for my illness in Dalhousie was confirmed by the doctor at the palace. My weakness and faintness was happening from the most natural cause in the world. I was to have a child!

Chapter Nine

Now that I was busy with preparations for my approaching motherhood, I thought perhaps my husband would occupy himself with something equally mature. I had hoped that eventually he would take an interest in the state and persuade the maharaja to give him a post in the government, but as time went on he seemed less and less inclined.

More than ever he sat brooding, bored with life and himself. I wanted to help him but I was feeling ill from my pregnancy. Seventeen was undoubtedly too young for motherhood and I was an immature seventeen. I wanted to be taken care of, myself; I did not feel up to coping with his problems.

But he would not leave me alone and bitterly resented the fact that I did not pay enough attention to him. "I'm sorry," I told him. "But you know I am not well."

"What does that have to do with it?" he asked coldly. "That is a long way off. Am I not to stay with you again until our child is born?"

He could not realize how ill I was. There was no way I could make him understand how I felt. He was not mature enough to accept any of life's inconveniences. When things went badly he was destroyed. He did not want me to be ill, not only because he loved me, but also because he did not want me to be dependent on him. In some ways, too, he resented the fact that I was going to have a baby. He wanted to have all the attention paid to him; he did not want to share my affection with anyone.

The months of my pregnancy were exhausting both physically and emotionally. I tried to be in good spirits but the constant struggle against my illness depressed me and the effort needed to keep our marriage going happily was too much for me.

Everyone in Kapurthala hoped that our child would be a boy so that the maharaja would have an heir in the second generation, but all along I had a feeling that it was going to be a girl. I was not surprised, then, when a baby girl was born to me. But the maharaja and my husband could not conceal their disappointment. My husband, however, quickly learned to love her, for little Indira was a beautiful baby.

Perhaps because of my illness during the pregnancy, Indira was not very strong. I was only able to nurse her for three weeks when I fell ill again and a wet nurse was brought in. Still Indira did not gain weight nor make any progress and the doctors prescribed a new diet of donkey's milk. By this time we were all frightened. Instead of growing fat and healthy Indira was wasting away. At five months she weighed only three and a half pounds.

The best doctors and nurses in India were brought in to make her well but she seemed to be dying before our eyes. All sorts of medicines were tried but nothing helped.

One evening as I was weeping with sorrow while preparing for bed an old ayah who had been in the Kapurthala family for forty years crept into my room.

"*Andata,*" * she said, looking around to make sure no one was coming, "do not listen to those red-faced people who know nothing about Indian babies. They are starving the child and she will die soon if something is not done about it."

I stopped crying for a moment and looked into the wrinkled old face of the ayah. She was an ignorant peasant woman. What could she know about saving my baby's life? But I listened anyway.

"That nurse is killing your baby," she whispered. "You must send her away at once."

I could not believe this because the nurse was a devoted and clever woman. She was doing everything medically possible to help cure my baby. I knew, too, how jealous Indian ayahs are of Europeans and that the nurse was resented by the whole household. Yet, in my desperation, I was ready to clutch at any straw.

"What would you do if I were to send them all away?" I asked, wondering what strange remedy the old woman could have in mind.

* Giver of food.

"I would get a young she-goat with her first kid," the ayah replied promptly. "I would feed it with special grass and herbs, milk it twice a day and give the milk to your baby."

I started to question her further but the woman began to scurry from the room. There were voices in the corridor.

"They must not see me here," she whispered in a frightened voice. "I will go now but if you want to save your baby, do as I say." Then she hurried from the room.

It sounded simple enough but we had already tried almost everything. The doctors and nurse objected violently to the old woman's suggestion. They were feeding Indira several medicines and warned me that dire things could happen if they stopped because there was so little strength left in the baby. But I had to take a chance.

Finally, they agreed to follow the advice of the ayah for one week. The goat was brought to the palace and placed under the supervision of the peasant woman. Every few hours Indira was fed the milk of the goat.

Within a few days Indira began to improve and by the end of the week she had gained twelve ounces. I was overcome with gratitude and happiness and the whole palace rejoiced with me. Indira was kept on goat's milk and steadily improved, growing stronger each day. In another five months she was a healthy baby and weighed over fourteen pounds. The old ayah beamed with pleasure at her success and, I'm afraid, gloated when the European nurse was sent away.

My husband and I spent much time in Simla and I preferred it to the other hill stations in India. Now that I was feeling better I wanted a little more gaiety. Simla, in those days, was more social than most places.

At the time, Lord Hardinge was viceroy and he and Lady Hardinge, who had known me as a schoolgirl in Paris, were very kind to me. As it happened, I needed their kindness.

It was not possible for me to behave like a subdued Indian woman after my European education. As a result I was resented by all of Simla, both Indians and Europeans. For one thing, I could see no reason why I had to keep purdah. I did not believe in it nor was I forced into it by my father-in-law who thought it a medieval custom. I wanted to be an ordinary human being as I had been in France and could not see why every time I shopped or attended a party or theater I had to be subjected to a barrage of criticism. I did not want to be a prisoner.

The only place where I felt welcome was at the viceregal lodge. Lady Hardinge was a great lady and His Excellency both an aristocrat and a wise human. They were always glad to see me and it was the one place I was really at home.

Simla, however, was not only the summer home of the viceregal court; it was also the summer seat of the Punjab government and its governor. The governor at the time was Sir Michael O'Dwyer and his attitude toward me and all Indians was far different from that of Lord and Lady Hardinge.

The fact that I was accepted by Simla society seemed to irritate the O'Dwyers. They were extremely prejudiced against the Indians and went out of their way to be malicious to me in an effort, I imagine, to show me that I was overstepping my bounds. I could not see that I was doing any wrong; my chief fault seemed to be that I refused to shut myself up at home both day and night.

One evening I accompanied Lady Hardinge to a concert at the Gaiety Theater as her guest. After the performance we walked together to the door, where Her Excellency kissed me good-by (as was her usual custom), entered her carriage, and drove off. A few moments later my rickshaw arrived and I left for home.

The next morning I received an official letter from the governor of Punjab. It was "observed with regret," stated the letter, that I had left the theater before Lady O'Dwyer —of whose position and seniority I must be aware.

My first impulse was to tear the letter to shreds and ignore the whole incident. I was shaking with anger as I thought it over. I hadn't even known that Lady O'Dwyer was in the theater. In any case, the letter and the emphasis on such a trivial incident had another meaning. It was in the nature of a warning to me. It was a letter telling me that I didn't know my place, a letter which clearly revealed the O'Dwyers' feelings about Indians. But I knew that I could not ignore the letter—some answer was required. It was not myself alone I was thinking of. I had to put aside my own feelings and humiliation and remember that the Tika Raja and I were representing our own government. I answered courteously that I was certainly aware of Lady O'Dwyer's seniority but that I had been completely unaware of her presence in the theater on the stated evening.

But Sir Michael had just begun his campaign of embarrassment. Shortly after this incident my husband received a letter from the governor. It had been "observed with regret" that we were using a title to which we had no right by calling ourselves Crown Prince and Crown Princess of Kapurthala. The fact was that Crown Prince is a literal English translation of Tika Raja and the newspapers had been using the title when they referred to us. We ourselves had never used it either officially or unofficially.

My husband answered in a formal and restrained note that their complaint would be more properly addressed to the editors of the newspapers in question. But he was hurt by the snub and a year later when we returned to Europe the newspapers both in France and England were informed that we did not wish to be referred to in such a fashion even though we were entitled to such an appellation in translating our Indian title.

Our lack of fear only infuriated Governor O'Dwyer further but there was not much he could do about it. If he could have had his secret wish answered perhaps he would have banished us from India forever but officially he was forced to accept our presence. It was even necessary that he invite us to certain official occasions.

When Lord Hardinge, on his retirement as viceroy, was given a large farewell banquet by the governor, we were naturally invited since there was no way he could exclude us. But even then he tried to create another incident to humiliate us. This time he was not so successful.

Etiquette decreed that after dinner each woman guest in leaving the hall should curtsey deeply to Lord Hardinge before withdrawing. Since I was wearing an Indian sari I did not curtsey but bowed. The next day there was an official letter from the governor.

Again "it was observed with regret" that I had shown a lack of respect towards the viceroy by not curtseying as expected. This time I answered indignantly. The viceroy had requested that I wear a sari rather than European dress since I was to be the only Indian woman present. A curtsey in Indian dress was not only out of place, it was also a physical impossibility. Furthermore, I continued, Lord Hardinge had approved such a bow to the extent that I had rehearsed it several times in his presence. I said nothing further in the letter and it was written with the utmost politeness.

But it did not end the hostilities between us. A week or two later Lord Hardinge invited me to lunch with him in Delhi. There were only a few of us at lunch and when the meal was over Lord Hardinge, pretending to frown, took me by the arm and announced that he wanted an interview with me alone in his office.

"At last, it is the guillotine," I murmured to Lord Hardinge.

He did not answer but looked at me, seriously; I could see the twinkle in his eye, however, and the smile he was trying so hard to suppress.

When he had shut the door carefully behind us in the office he broke into laughter. Then he pointed to his desk.

"Brinda, my dear," he said, smiling broadly. "I have here a very large file about a very small girl. It is an official document from the Punjab government."

He told me that my every move had been watched and recorded. There were pages and pages, he said, about my not curtseying, about my reasons for not curtseying, and about all my "sins" which I had committed toward Sir Michael and his government. It was not so amusing at the time, but it is funny to recollect today that my various offenses of a social nature were added up by this fanatical man to imply that there was something subversive about a young girl who had failed to observe the proper social amenities.

The last notation was written by Lord Hardinge as I sat next to his desk watching. It was a curt line which dismissed the file and the compilation of incidents.

It was the last time I was bothered by the O'Dwyers. After that we limited our contacts with each other as much as was feasible. I accepted their official invitations only when it seemed absolutely necessary; on their part they stopped observing or commenting on my conduct.

To be a conqueror is a delicate trust and the misuse of such power can bring tragedy to both sides. Unfortunately, the chance for power brings people into such offices who want to use it for their own aggrandizement. For every kind and wise Lord Hardinge who ruled in India, there were more men like Sir Michael who misused such power. The unfortunate results of such misuse have already been seen in the years past and was more than partly responsible for the hatred which grew between India and England.

For more than three years after our marriage the Tika Raja and I remained in India. Most of our time was spent in Kapurthala and Simla with occasional visits to Kashmir and Mussoorie. We both adored our child, Indira, and took her everywhere we went, for I refused to leave her to the care of servants.

In fact, Indira was the strongest link between us. As difficult as the beginning of our marriage had been, it had grown increasingly worse with the passage of time. The Tika Raja was more depressed than ever. He had long black moods of silence where he would sit for hours without doing anything. Sometimes for days he would not speak to me except in monosyllables.

Clichés hold much truth; that is how they become clichés. "Love breeds love" was a good one in our case. It is difficult to go on loving where there is no love in return and I found that tolerance began to be the most that I could give my husband. On his part he was very jealous of me and accused me constantly of not paying enough attention to him and his needs. But he showed me very little affection and no understanding. I was trying my best but it was a grim ordeal. There was no happiness in it for either of us.

Sometimes in my desperation and loneliness I thought of divorce but such a thing was not possible in India. Even today, except in one or two states such as Baroda, unhappy marriages cannot be dissolved. For women, even after the death of their husbands, cannot always remarry. In most places widows are forced to remain alone for the rest of their lives.

But I could not resign myself to a life of misery. I was still young enough to hope that someday everything would be all right and eager enough to try to work out a solution to give us as much happiness as possible.

I was still longing to return to France. There I had found the most happiness I had known in my life. Perhaps, I thought that, if we could both live in Europe, we could find joy there together. The Tika Raja was excited by the idea, as well, for he loved travel and was more than willing to leave India. For three years, however, the maharaja flatly refused to allow us to leave and it was not until the summer of 1914 when I flatly refused to go to Simla or Mussoorie that he reluctantly gave us permission to spend the summer in France.

I was wild with excitement. In my innocence about life I believed in the magic of places. I thought that by moving to another spot you left your problems behind. I did not know then that you must bring your happiness with you. There is no magic island, no matter how the sun sparkles on the water or how gentle the breeze, which can give you a peace of mind you do not possess yourself. There is an old Hindu proverb which says that a man in a crowded slum can be more alone than one on an isolated hilltop. It is the same thing with happiness. If you do not bring it with you, it is not there.

Once the maharaja relented he was most generous in the provisions he made for our trip. If his heir was going to Europe he must go in the traditional style of the Maharaja of Kapurthala. He objected at first to our taking Indira along but I insisted and my husband backed me up. We loved her too much to be separated from her even for a few months. Finally, the maharaja gave in to that, too, and we started off on our trip accompanied by a number of servants.

Paris in the spring of 1914 was one the gayest social seasons of the century and I, after my years of dullness and misery in India, found it doubly exciting. We stayed at a hotel on the Champs Élysées and all my old friends vied with each other to invite us to parties. Night after night we danced and were gay at balls and parties. I loved every minute of it from the moment of dressing for the ball to the waltzing and laughter of the party.

But instead of being cheered up by the gaiety the Tika Raja was more unhappy than ever. He was often jealous when I danced with any other man at parties.

In July we crossed the channel to London but the atmosphere there was depressing. There was nothing but war talk. Like our Parisian friends we were tired by talk of war and refused to take it seriously. We made many friends in London and the Tika Raja cheered up considerably; it was as though we were on a second honeymoon. The sounds of war began to be more ominous but we did not want to change our plans and returned to Paris at the end of July.

On our return to Paris I saw Guy. It had been more than five years since our last meeting but when we were together it was almost as if we had never been apart.

From inside his army jacket he took out a golden coin I had given him years before.

"I may go into battle any day now," he said soberly, "but I will always keep this with me as part of you."

My eyes filled with tears as we said good-by. He kissed my

hand once tenderly and I watched his blond head disappear out the door. I never saw him again. But years later his brother came to see me to give me back the worn Indian coin. They had taken it from Guy's body as he lay on the field of battle in 1916.

We were staying once again at the Hotel Astoria. Paris seemed just the same as it had been when we left it except that it was August now and the city steamed from the summer heat. Then suddenly everything was changed. It was August 4, 1914. War had been declared.

Chapter Ten

After the war broke out the Hotel Astoria, which was under German management, was closed down by the police at once. We tried frantically to find another hotel for ourselves and our three servants but there were no accommodations available. Since my husband was feeling ill it was up to me to solve these problems.

I had no experience to help me. We were practically stranded in Paris and although we had many friends there I knew that it would be necessary for us to leave since the country was at war. Then I realized that we were under British Protectorate and that the embassy would help us.

The British Embassy took the problem out of my hands at once. They insisted that we leave France immediately for London and arranged passports and visas for our departure. We still took the fact of war lightly and I assured the Tika Raja, who was as ignorant of politics as I, that all the trouble would be over in a few weeks. I was so convinced that it would all blow over that I persuaded Princesse de Broglie to store our luggage for a few weeks. I assured her that we would soon return to claim it.

It was just as hot in London as it had been in Paris and we stifled from the heat. My husband was not well enough to remain in London so we went to several seaside resorts. It could scarcely have been called a vacation. The Tika Raja was confined to bed most of the time. And little Indira was cross and fretful from the heat and the change in climate. I was restless and depressed by the English hotels and the incredibly bad food. The stoicism of the English has always seemed remarkable to me and I thought then that their ability to ignore poor cooking, particularly after the food of France, was the most remarkable feat of all.

We began to realize as time went on that the war was not going to be over in a matter of weeks. Furthermore, we received letters from the India Office which suggested strongly that we return to India. The Tika Raja was glad enough to go back home after spending some days in London where we waited for our baggage to be sent from Paris. We sailed for India.

We spent the war years in India at our home in Kapurthala, in Poona and Kashmir. After my bad experiences in Simla we avoided it especially since my dear friends, the Hardinges, were no longer there.

My husband was delighted to learn that I was going to have another child, and both he and his father, the maharaja, hoped that it would be a boy and heir to the state.

But again they were bitterly disappointed. Once more the baby was a girl. I loved her. She was both a pretty baby and a happy one, and I could not understand why they were making such a fuss over my failure to produce a son.

I was still only a young girl myself; I wanted to have more children. I had plenty of hope that sooner or later I would bear a son. Indira was a sweet child and the new baby girl was a delight to me. I was even happier when some months after her birth I found that again I was going to have another child. In many ways I was more content than I had been in the earlier days of my marriage. Bearing children had fulfilled a deep need in me and had now given me an outlet for my affection in caring for my children. I have often thought that nature has been kinder to women than to men in this way. They are able to find more solace for their disappointment in life through children.

This time I wanted a boy. I was sure that the third time would have to be lucky. But when the nurse brought the baby, wrapped in a soft blanket, and placed it in my arms, she whispered, "You have borne a beautiful little girl."

I turned my head away and cried out, "Take her away!" I was so disappointed not only for myself but for my husband. The Tika Raja, however was kind and tried to console me, but for weeks I was depressed. My father-in-law was inconsolable, however, and he could not conceal his contempt for me.

It is easy to understand the value of bringing a male child into the Indian world. The position of women in India is still such a subservient one that girl babies are thought to be of little value. With a male it is quite different especially with a male of royal blood. Then the world is his for the asking.

The blame for not bearing a male heir is usually put on the woman although I have since learned that physiologically the choice of sex is determined by the male. In any case the maharaja did not bother to pretend that he was not angry over my failure to produce a son.

We named the baby Ourmila. I soon got over my own disappointment and loved this baby as much as the others. In my heart it had not really made a difference; I only wanted to do my duty and please my husband and father-in-law. Girls seemed easier to bring up anyway and secretly I thought they often turned out better in the long run.

India had its own hardships in those years although they could not be blamed on the war. It was only that living there was on a more primitive basis than our life in Europe.

The heat of an Indian summer is really unbearable so that as the spring departed we quickly went into the cool hills to spend the hottest months of the year. One summer we took a bungalow in Poona in the Nilgiri Hills. There was very little to do there and we usually went to bed early.

One night about midnight I woke up screaming with pain and terror. Something had attacked me while I slept. I was in excruciating pain and as I sat up in bed I howled for help. My husband rushed about trying to locate a candle, crying all the while that I was being murdered.

At first my whole body seemed consumed with pain; then I could feel that it was coming from my right hand. When the candle was lit we saw that blood was pouring from a gash in my finger. My night dress was soaked with it and the bed was covered with blood as well.

The first thing we thought of was snakes since there were many poisonous ones lurking in the garden. I rocked on the bed clutching a towel to my finger.

"I am going to die," I wailed. "I know it, this is the end. I am dying of poison."

The Tika Raja was in a frenzy. He did not know whether to stay and comfort me or whether to rush for a doctor. Finally he composed himself enough to send a servant for aid and sat by my bed moaning with me. We were both sure that death was just a breath away.

The only one who had her wits about her was my old ayah. In searching about the room for the cause of my accident she found a broken plate under the bed, surrounded by half-eaten biscuits. One of the servants had placed it there, the biscuits sprinkled with poison to kill rats which had been entering the house. It was a rat, then, not a snake which had bitten my finger.

I sank back on the bed in relief and exhaustion. My death was not yet so close at hand.

The next morning eight large rats were found dead in the garden. But I had had enough of such living. By afternoon the servants had packed our belongings and we motored to Bombay where we could find some semblance of civilization again.

Civilization is hardly the word to describe a visit we made to the state of Hyderabad in 1916. I had already seen much luxury in my life but even I was staggered at the scale on which our host, the Nizam, lived.

The Nizam was the wealthiest man on earth and India's top Moslem ruler. A man of medium height, unassuming manner, and simple dress he would have passed unnoticed in any gathering. But his tastes in living were not quite so simple.

We had been invited for a three-day visit and were lodged in a palace for special guests. An elaborate program for our visit had been mapped out for us as in some ways it was a state visit. My husband and I had accompanied one of his brothers and a stepbrother, as well as a small group of officials. The Nizam was a busy man and we did not expect to see much of him.

On the first day, however, he invited us to lunch with him and gave me a place of honor next to him at the table. He seemed fascinated by the fact that I had lived abroad many years; he had heard, no doubt unfavorably, that I had become completely Westernized. He asked a thousand questions and listened attentively to my answers.

The Nizam had something of a forbidding reputation but I enjoyed talking to him and answered his questions freely. He seemed somewhat dismayed by my independence and more than once I caught him looking at me and back at the other Indian women as if to say, "This is what *all* our women will come to if we give them a chance."

I could not help but be amused by his attitude and probably out of my own rebellion tried to seem even more emancipated than I was. We talked all through luncheon and when it was over and my husband and I were back in our own apartments where we expected to dine, we received a message that the Nizam had been so delighted with his guests from Kapurthala that he requested their presence at dinner as well. Once again I sat beside the Nizam and we talked at length about my life in India and France.

Early the next morning the servants of the Nizam brought us trays piled high with gifts of silk and gold materials, golden trinkets, flowers, fruits, and garlands of gold thread. In order that our servants' food might be prepared exactly to their liking and religious requirements, sheep and goats, chickens, eggs, grains, etc., were given to them.

The following evening a banquet was given in our honor in the Nizam's famous palace. As I was dressing for the party, an official of the palace appeared, followed by a servant bearing a tray on which lay a magnificent necklace of diamonds, emeralds, and pearls. I gasped when I saw it but made no move to take it from the tray.

The messenger bowed deeply. "It is a small gift from His Highness," he said.

"Oh," I exclaimed, putting my hand to my mouth, "I cannot accept such a valuable necklace."

"His Highness would be deeply offended if you returned it," insisted his envoy.

"You must take it back at once," I answered, looking at it once more as the servant held it before me.

But my protest were to no avail. The Nizam's envoy could not be prevailed upon to take back the gift and he persuaded me that I would be insulting his emperor if I did not accept gracefully what he termed the Nizam's "hospitality"! So I kept the necklace and wore it that evening to the dinner party. To my husband and his brothers the

Nizam sent each one a set of diamond buttons and a beautiful gold watch.

When we arrived at the palace I discovered that I was the only woman present. The room was crowded with men and it seemed that nearly all of Hyderabad's nobility was gathered there. The men were dressed in sparkling brocade with high-collared jackets which reached to the knees and buttoned with pearls or diamonds, tight-fitting white trousers. It was a glittering sight.

At first I was dumb with shyness in the midst of all these men but the Nizam presented me to the company, then took my arm and accompanied me into the dining salon where I sat at his right. As I took my seat he leaned over and whispered in my ear.

"I wanted you to enjoy the party," he said, "so I only invited a few people."

I looked around the table. There were more than seventy people in the room.

When the dinner was over the Nizam presented to each guest of the Kapurthala party seven golden Hyderabadi coins which came from his own mint as a souvenir of our visit. Then after coffee was served the servants brought in several large gold boxes studded with diamonds and emeralds in which were cigars and cigarettes. His Highness offered me a cigarette, then cigars were given to the Kapurthala princes.

Then the Nizam took up a handful of cigarettes and flung them into the faces of some of the nobles in his court. I looked up in surprise. But the princes who had received the cigarettes were smiling and the ones who had not looked disappointed. Later I learned that only the nobles the Nizam considered worthy could smoke in his presence. Throwing cigarettes across a dinner table seemed a gesture to me but it turned out to be an invariable custom of the Nizam. It was probably a hang-over from the days when rulers were considered above the rules of manners.

His Highness talked to me at some length about Europe. He had never been there and was eager to see something of the world outside of India.

"Oh, you would love France," I said eagerly. "If only I can return there soon."

"I would like to make the trip," he said soberly, "but I am told it will be too much of an expense."

My eyes opened wide. I looked about the dining room which was lavishly appointed and at the gold plates and jewels all about us. The Nizam saw my astonishment.

"You see," he answered my unspoken question (for I knew he was the richest man in the world), "they tell me that since I must go as the ruler of Hyderabad I must have my proper retinue."

"But surely you could afford to go around the world many times," I protested.

"Yes, I can afford it," he sighed, "but it is expensive. My advisors tell me that it will cost fifteen crores."

My head swam as I computed the cost. Fifteen crores in English money was ten million pounds or about forty million dollars in American money.

The Nizam laughed with delight when he saw my stricken face. "It is quite a lot of money, is it not, my dear?" he said.

As we rose from the table the Nizam announced to his guests that he was going to show me the palace. He gave me his arm and together we walked from the dining salon.

Then the Nizam led me along dark endless corridors which twisted and turned and wound about through the palace. We walked silently up and down long flights of stairs, through curved archways and carved doorways. The corridors apparently had little use for they smelled musty.

The dimness was beginning to bother my eyes, for the corridors were poorly lit. I shivered a little from the dampness. Where was he taking me? I wondered. Perhaps my husband would be angry because I had gone alone with the Nizam.

At last we came to a doorway. It looked out on an enormous courtyard in which a fleet of motor cars were parked. There were rows and rows of long, sleek limousines all with blinds which were drawn. I looked at the Nizam in wonder and was about to ask him what the cars were for when he drew me past the courtyard and into a room almost the size of the ballroom at Buckingham Palace. When I saw what was in that room my question fled from my lips. I could only stand in the doorway and gasp at the sight before my eyes.

There, before me, standing practically at attention stood over two hundred women. All were lovely-looking with dark eyes, slim supple bodies, and golden skin which shone like satin. They were exquisitely dressed in sparkling brocades and shimmering silks, and gold bangles and jeweled bracelets on their arms and wrists. They were undoubtedly the most beautiful women I had ever seen.

I drew back in embarrassment. I did not want to go into the room. So this was what a harem was like! I had heard many times about them and had often wished I could see one close at hand but I had no idea what a shock it would be to come face to face with the hundreds of wives of one man.

The Nizam took my arm firmly. "Come along," he said. "I want my wives to see you."

He led me past rows and rows of these dazzling women. They looked at me curiously but little of any other expression passed over their faces. They did not look at the Nizam nor did they speak to him. He spoke to no one.

I was vastly relieved when we left the room and made our way back to the rest of the company. I could not help asking some questions.

"How many wives do you have?" I asked the Nizam.

"There are about two hundred and fifty," he answered, "although I am not sure of the exact number."

In some way I felt that it had been wrong of the Nizam to show off his wives like a herd of cattle. Perhaps they had been hurt or offended by my presence.

I couldn't contain myself any longer. "Why did you take me there?" I burst out. "It seemed unfair to them."

The Nizam smiled indulgently at me. "I took you there," he answered, "because I wanted to give my wives a little treat. They have so little to occupy themselves; they like to see a strange face once in a while."

When we returned to the rest of the guests I told the Tika Raja's stepbrother that I had seen the Nizam's harem.

"Does it not seem incredible to you?" I asked.

"His grandfather had three thousand wives," he answered. "Even his father had eight hundred. You see, in comparison, the Nizam is a very modest man."

"Does he have many children?"

"He seems to have more wives than children," he said. "He has only eighty sons and sixty daughters."

I could not forget the sight of those women herded together. All evening long I was staggered by the recollection of the hundreds of women who were kept confined and closely guarded. It was worse than prison. What could they do with their time? Did they just while away their lives, concealed in that one room and in those long limousines with the shades pulled down?

I shuddered when I thought by what narrow margin I had escaped being born into such a fate. And yet, as I mulled it over, I began to realize that every way of life has its problems. Where there is freedom there is also responsibility. Where there is dependence there is also protection. I would have been horrified at the idea of having a job or working to support myself; these women would have been completely incapable of it. At least they were well taken care of; they had to solve no problems for themselves. I began to see that there is more than one way to look at anything.

The following evening, after a small dinner party, the Nizam played for us on the *thabla*, a small, tightly strung drum which is said to be capable of producing more than four hundred musical tones. He was a master of the instrument and was reputed to be one of the finest technicians of the art in all India. He was accompanied by a small string orchestra. The sharp light tones of the music were a delight to hear and he played for quite a while that evening.

Not long afterward we left Hyderabad. We made an official state visit to Mysore, a lovely tropical land whose lush emerald forests make it almost an incongruity in India. Mysore was far different from Hyderabad.

The Maharaja of Mysore had little desire for the treasures of the world. A dreamy, soft-spoken man, he was deeply spiritual and poetic. It was impossible not to recognize his goodness and wisdom at once even though his manner was completely quiet and unassuming.

The maharaja was a serious, progressive man with a sense of responsibility toward his subjects. He had probably done more for his state than any other ruler in India. Mysore was the first state to have its own constitution and although the British government had forced the state to sign its gold fields over to them, depriving the state of about fifteen million dollars yearly, the maharaja had been making great strides forward in an effort to bring up the backward country. He had already developed public services, including medical care, and had built hundreds of miles of perfect roads through the sandalwood forests of Mysore.

The Maharaja of Mysore sent us down to the mines, showed us through clinics, and motored over the newly built roads with us. The contrast to Hyderabad was great and I saw how much good can be accomplished by a ruler who wants to help his people.

We spent the long years of war going from place to place in India. We could not settle in Kapurthala because the situation was too uncomfortable there. Both the Tika Raja and I were restless and every attempt on our parts, particularly mine, to do anything constructive, was frustrated by the maharaja. So we wandered about the country but in the back of our minds was always the hope that when war stopped raging in Europe we could return there to live.

We spent the summer of 1918 in Kashmir. It was a peaceful time and by then I was willing to trade such peace for happiness. We lived a simple life there with little social activity but we made a number of new friends whom I liked very much.

Among them was the Consul General of Persia, Sir Dawood Khan. He was somewhat of an expert in astrology and since I had much interest in the same subject we spent many hours together discussing the validity of horoscopes and astrology.

I teased him to tell me when he thought the war would be over. At first he did not want to say but he knew how anxious I was to know and how desperately I wanted to return to Europe. Finally, he gave in and consulted long charts of moons and suns rising and falling.

"The war will be over this year," he told me.

"Are you just saying it to make me happy?" I asked him. "Please tell me."

He shook his head. "It will be finished this year," he repeated.

I hoped he was right. I wanted to pack immediately and go down to the plains. Perhaps everything was already over. I persuaded the Tika Raja to leave, but while we were still making plans a terrible epidemic of influenza broke out and thousands and thousands of people died in but a few days. We were advised to remain in Kashmir for the children's sakes.

Because of the epidemic we stayed there throughout the fall months. Then the good news reached us that the Armistice had been signed and the war was over. Everyone was grateful to hear the news but I, more than most Indians, was overjoyed to know that my dear adopted country, France, was at long last free of war.

I wanted to go to France at once; it would have been like going home but it was not possible just then. The Tika Raja and I spent Christmas in Gwalior and then returned to our own state of Kapurthala.

Chapter Eleven

We remained in Kapurthala during the year of 1919. My father-in-law left for Europe in March and my husband was acting as regent during his absence. India was by no means serene following World War I; there was much unrest in the country. Mahatma Gandhi had started a nation-wide political movement and in our own state the Sikhs and Moslems were rioting. But my husband handled his responsibilities well and averted what could have been a political crisis in the state.

There was little for me to do. The maharaja had left strict orders that I was to have no part in any affairs of state. Nor was it acceptable that I give my time to charity. By specific instruction of the maharaja I was to remain idle. He did not believe that a woman should occupy herself with any but family duties.

Bored and restless during the long months we were

forced to remain in Kapurthala with nothing to do, I yearned to go back to my beloved Paris. My husband was anxious to return there, too, and when his father came back in 1920 we were able to get his consent to leave almost at once. In fact, the maharaja decided to accompany us, at least as far as Marseille.

Our plans included taking our three young daughters but when we reached Bombay we discovered that our second little girl, Sushila, had developed measles. In a day or two Indira and Ourmila followed suit. The doctors, of course, would not hear of their making the trip to Europe. I was worried about the children and wanted to return to Kapurthala with them but the maharaja would not let me. He insisted that I make the trip to Europe. I did not want to leave the girls and begged to stay in India for much as I wanted to go to Europe I preferred to see that my babies were all right.

In the end I had to give in. The children were taken back to Kapurthala by their governess and servants and we sailed for France. It was difficult for me to reconcile myself to leaving without them. In the long months of enforced idleness in Kapurthala I had devoted most of my time to the children. All my energy had been absorbed in their care and baby problems. Now suddenly I was separated from them.

The first few days at sea I was miserable. I walked the decks hour after hour or sat in a chair staring out at the dark water. The prospect of spending months away from my children was torturous. It was like losing part of myself. For comfort I turned back to my sacred Hindu book, the

Gita, and tried to find consolation in the words of my religion. The words of comfort were there but it was not so easy to feel better only for the asking. Such words are not like a drug which can be taken to perform miracles. There is struggle in religion as well as anywhere else.

Surrender everything to God, I read, detach yourself from the things of the world, expect nothing in return for your efforts. Intellectually, I believed the words of the Gita. I saw that what I had been doing with my children was wrong. I had become so absorbed in them that I wanted to possess them and I realized how selfish it is to want to own another human being. My children could not help but be hurt by me if I continued.

And yet it is easy enough to know what is right. Emotionally I could not accept such a philosophy. I loved my children and needed them and the separation was a hardship. There was no way I could pretend to what I did not feel.

It was obvious that I was not ready to renounce the world and all I held dear. I was torn with conflict. On the one I wanted to become pure in heart and follow the path of goodness; on the other hand I still yearned for the pleasures of life. I was not ready to make the choice.

It was easier to put aside the Gita for the moment and forget my pain in the pursuit of pleasure. Perhaps someday I would be mature enough to be content with the satisfactions of the spirit but not just yet.

Most things you dread usually turn out well. The children made an excellent recovery and were soon running about. They did not miss us but went off to Mussoorie for the summer with their governesses where they were in the best of spirits. To them, being without their parents meant only a lark and a chance to be mischievous without as much punishment.

At Marseille, the maharaja left us and my husband and I continued on to Paris where we were met at the station by my dearest friend, Beatrix de Pracomtal. Beatrix and I squealed with delight to see each other just as we had done in the years we were schoolmates together in Paris.

Our meeting was tinged with sadness when Beatrix told me her news. She had lost her brother in the war and her husband, Count Robert Meunier de Hussoy, had been crippled for life.

Everywhere I went it was the same story. Nearly all of my friends had suffered some bereavement. The loss of young men in France was tragic; everywhere young women and mothers wore their sad badge of mourning.

We stayed at the Ritz and I spent the first few weeks renewing old friendships and shopping on the Champs Élysées. Paris had changed. It was a sad city now, clouded by death, and there was an air of resignation which made it seem far different from the gay city I had remembered.

As spring grew into summer, however, Paris seemed to change. Slowly it was becoming an international city. Most of the newcomers were Americans. They all had money to spend and seemed intent on spending it as fast as possible.

It brought a sudden jolt of prosperity to the war-damaged city. Night clubs began doing a boom business; theaters and music halls had long lines of impatient people waiting outside to buy tickets. More and more restaurants took down their shutters, repainted the walls, and doubled their prices.

There was a new word in vogue, "jazz," and clusters of smoke-filled night clubs began to open along the small side streets of Paris. Visitors from abroad and Parisians themselves soon crowded the small clubs to listen to this new kind of music. It was irresistible and it was not enough merely to listen to jazz—the new music had to be danced to and soon it was the rage of France.

At first a certain snobbery among the social set kept them away. Jazz? That was for the tourists, mainly the Americans. But before long the younger set was wild over the new craze and they flocked into the cafés. I must confess that I was one of them. From the first moment I heard it I was captivated by what we laughingly termed that "barbaric music" and was determined that I would learn to dance it as well as the agile Americans who were masters of the art.

The Tika Raja objected to my taking dance lessons at first but for the past months I had been so depressed that when he saw my enthusiasm for the new craze he gave in. It was probably good for me at the time because it took my mind off my children. For the moment I could fling myself into dancing and I did so with more abandon, perhaps, than was befitting the wife of a future maharaja.

The gaiety was hard to resist, particularly after my years of quiet during the war in India but even I was shocked at the pitch of living in Paris in those days. Money was flung about as if it had no meaning at all and to the Parisians, who have some frugality no matter how wealthy they are, the Americans and South Americans, freely throwing about their money as if it had no value, were a strange and weird new species.

Money was at a premium to the French. Most of the aristocracy there had lost much of their wealth in the last few years and had seen little of the prewar lavishness they had known. Now strangers from other lands were trying to buy their way into Parisian society. The foreigners entertained extravagantly. There were thousands of orchids, caviar, and the finest champagne flowing at every party. Jazz orchestras were brought from America; the finest chefs in France were hired to make a party successful. Eventually the French succumbed. If the Americans wanted to court their favor, why not? The price for acceptance in society was soon set.

From Paris we moved on to Deauville which was then at the height of its popularity, and the feverish gaiety which possessed all of Paris seemed to have found its way there along with the people who fled from the city as the summer heat descended. But we were restless there, too. I was still nervous and somewhat depressed and only the constant round of parties and balls could keep me from thinking about India and the problems that I could not solve.

A month later we moved on to Venice where we stayed at the Lido which was just beginning to be fashionable. There was even more frantic pursuit of pleasure in Venice, with everyone trying to outdo each other in larger, splashier parties. I was captivated by the Italians, few of whom I had met before. They seemed more natural than the French, less sophisticated, and far less disillusioned.

The sands of the Lido stretch endlessly along the blue waters of the sea. I was enchanted by the beauty of Italy and loved sitting on the golden sands, hour after hour. I watched the water with longing as I had learned to love it so in the holy city of Hardwar when I was a child, but I still could not get used to the idea of what seemed to me a shameless style of bathing dress.

Today, those old-fashioned bathing suits would make a modern girl laugh with their modesty of cut but then I was horrified at exposing myself to that extent. It was so much the vogue, however, that I could not resist buying one in a small shop in Venice. But I wore it under a long bathing coat and sat in the sun, huddled under my wraps. Nothing anyone could say would induce me to take off the coat and swim.

One morning while sitting on the beach with Prince Phillip of Hesse I noticed what I thought was an inflated mattress floating into shore. My eyesight was not perfect and I squinted to get a better look at it. I could not swim too well myself and thought if I could get over my shyness perhaps I could buy one of them to cling to.

I pointed it out to Prince Phillip.

"That's exactly what I need," I exclaimed. "If I had one of those huge pink things to support me I'd go in the water, too."

"Heavens," whispered the prince. "That's not a mattress. That's Elsa Maxwell!"

Hastily I grabbed for my glasses and looked again. There floating on the water was a large woman with a perfectly happy expression on her face. She seemed pleased with herself, and at that moment I decided that if she did not mind exposing herself to public view, then I had nothing to fear.

When she came out of the water, Prince Phillip called her over. I tried to hush him but he insisted on telling her the whole story. I blushed with embarrassment but Elsa Maxwell was a good-humored woman and laughed heartily.

"With my figure," she said, "anything would be shocking. So I just go ahead and wear what I please. I'm afraid it doesn't make much of a difference."

The most feared woman in Venice at that time was the Princesse Jane di San Faustino. Her whip-lash tongue was said to have killed more people socially than anything else in Europe. She seemed to take great pride in her power and it was said that she liked to see her victims squirm as she crushed them.

I was terrified the first time I met her. For weeks I had heard long tales about her viciousness. Since I liked parties and people, I was afraid that she might not like me and that if she said the word, I would be black-listed in Venice. The first time I met her I could barely speak. But she was a perceptive woman.

"You have nothing to be frightened about, my dear," she said.

I tried to compose myself and protest that I was not at all terrified but the princess interrupted me.

"They've told you dreadful stories about me," she said crisply. "And what's more," she added, "they're all true."

My mouth opened in astonishment.

"But there is nothing for you to worry about," she went on, smiling. "I like you and will try to help you."

And with that she put her arm on my shoulders and took me about the party to introduce me to the people she considered worth knowing. I never did feel too secure with her because I was always afraid that eventually she might attack me but during my entire visit to Venice she was kind and cordial and treated me as somewhat of a protégée.

I was beginning to feel better. Basking on the warm beaches in the day, dancing under the bright stars at night were beginning to relax me. I was able to forget everything in the days and nights of gaiety. But my husband was growing restless. It always seemed that when I was enjoying myself he was unhappy. I don't think he wanted me to be miserable but when I was depressed he seemed more confident and less insecure about me.

Like many wives, I never seemed to like his friends. I couldn't help feeling that he had a genius for picking out the strangest and least amusing people. And naturally he felt the same way about me. This I have since heard is apparently a common complaint of married couples all over the world.

But now he could not tolerate Venice another moment. He hated dancing and now could not even stand to watch others, any longer. I suggested that we return to Paris so that he might see some of his own friends and we went there. But we did not stay long. Once more the Tika Raja was bored and we moved on to Biarritz.

After a short stay in Biarritz it was time to go back to India. Our European vacation was over. The maharaja wanted us to come back home. I was happy to return in order to see my little girls and for once I had had enough excitement. Europe and its frenzied gaiety had left me exhausted. Perhaps after the quiet and peace of India I might be ready for more after a time, but for the moment I was content to be idle.

We remained in India for the next two years. Once again I tried to interest myself in charitable works but it almost always ended in a battle with the maharaja. I still wanted to help the poor; I had never been able to forget the hungry and desperate faces of the thousands of starving people I had for the first time seen on my honeymoon.

One of my plans was to try to stimulate interest in education. I was sure that with less illiteracy there would be faster progress in India. I made one suggestion to the schools in Kapurthala. I felt that the young women should remain in school until they were sixteen or seventeen, and offered money to the schools for prizes as an inducement to study for examinations.

But I was quickly condemned for trying to help. Not long after the competition had been announced, my father-in-law sent for me. I could see that he was not pleased.

"Reports have come to me," he said sternly, "that you have been interfering with the education of the young women in Kapurthala."

"Interfering?" I asked in amazement. "I have been trying to help them."

"Well, it is none of your affair," the maharaja said angrily. "I'm sick of hearing complaints about you. Why can't you leave things alone?"

I tried to explain that the purpose of the prizes was to give the young girls an incentive to continue their studies.

The maharaja banged his fist on the desk.

"That is exactly what the people object to," he exclaimed. "They say you are ruining their girls. They complain that you are filling their heads full of desires which cannot be fulfilled. Their parents want to marry them at twelve; they are not interested in your foolish ideas of education."

"Don't you see," I pleaded, "how wrong it is for those children of twelve to marry? They bear children too early and many of them die before they are twenty."

"That is no concern of yours," he said coldly. "Their parents are worried that if they do not marry young they will not be able to find husbands for them. Furthermore, they say that if young girls do not marry, they will get into trouble."

There was no way I could explain my point of view to the maharaja. My heart ached for the fragile young girls who married before maturity and immediately bore child after child. They were not strong enough to bear such burdens and often they became ill. I felt these children needed help and that education would teach them there was more to life than the pain and misery most of them knew.

I tried once more to plead my case before my father-in-law.

"Is it right," I asked, "for us to have so much when the people of our state have so little?"

The maharaja's face grew red. "What kind of talk is that?" he shouted. "You go too far. Do you dare to criticize the way I govern my state?"

I was sick of diplomacy.

"Yes, I do object," I retorted. "I have seen the hungry babies lying in filth and misery and their tortured parents who cannot feed them. It is wrong that we do not help these people."

The maharaja stood up. He glared at me in a fury of temper.

"How dare you meddle in my affairs?" he cried. "Your presumption is unbelievable. I do not need you to tell me what to do."

Wearily, I rose from my chair. There was nothing further to say. But the maharaja stopped me as I reached the door.

"I want no repetition of this," he said. "I have had enough of your impertinences. Next time sterner measures will be necessary."

I knew I had to be careful not to rouse his anger again. But I still wanted to help the people of India. What was the point of my education if I could not use what I had been taught? I knew certain reforms were necessary and saw the example of other rulers of states who were trying to bring some progress to their country.

Now that the maharaja was giving a small amount of responsibility to his son, I tried to discuss these problems with the Tika Raja. I pointed out that if factories were started in Kapurthala it would mean employment and food for the peasants. I couldn't help being honest in expressing what I felt. It was easy to see that the state was badly run. Since the maharaja did not take an active interest in the government but spent most of his time in travel, there was no order in the government. His ministers cheated him constantly and he never checked up on them or asked for an accounting.

But my husband was bored with my ideas. He was not interested in helping his people, either.

"You're always causing so much trouble, Brinda," he said. "Can't you keep quiet and forget all these ideas?"

But I could not. Secretly, I tried to continue my work. I organized clubs for women where they could come for some recreation and taught them to play hockey, croquet, and other games. Then I brought together a group of widows and found a place where they could spin and weave cloth to sell it. I was distressed by the plight of widows, for since they are not permitted to remarry when their husbands die, they have no means of support and many of them die of starvation. By organizing them as a group and bringing in an artisan to teach them the craft of weaving, the women were able to make enough money to pay for their food and shelter.

I was no longer afraid of my father-in-law's wrath. By this time I was old enough to realize that I myself had to take some responsibility in doing what I believed was right. My conscience would not allow me to sit back in the palace absorbed in my own life, eating, drinking, and dancing, while around me I saw wretched human beings dying like animals.

I did some work in the hospital and collected clothing and food to give to the poor. The people of Kapurthala began to know me and often while attending a function they would cry out for "Tika Rani." This infuriated the maharaja who would then accuse me of disobeying his orders.

Finally he grew so angry with me that he threatened to

exile both my husband and myself. The palace was agog with the news and gossip flew from one end of the court to the other. I heard all sorts of rumors.

"He will poison you," said one intimate, "if you are not careful. You have gone too far in provoking his anger."

I laughed carelessly. "Oh, he is not so bad as all that," I answered.

The Tika Raja was also becoming angry. He was tired of the endless arguments and since he wanted to get along with his father, at any price, insisted that I give up all my work and do as the maharaja had bidden me.

He did not help, however, to make things more peaceful. When he wanted something from his father, he did not hesitate to preface it with, "Brinda said that I should tell you this."

In the end, there was no way I could continue all the work I wanted to do. There was so much pressure from both the maharaja and my husband that I was forced to accede to their demands almost entirely.

I was bitterly disappointed. I felt there was so much to be done in our country and that, if there was a way in which I could be of help, it was not wrong to try.

As time went on I realized there was another reason behind the maharaja's insistence that we remain entirely out of his government. He realized that his neglect of his people and his own desire for personal luxury had not made him very popular in the state. An extremely egotistical man, he could not bear the thought that his son might achieve the popularity which he had never had.

And he had many reasons for disliking me. He resented

the fact that my background was more royal than his (even though this was the primary reason he wanted his son to marry me); he hated me for not giving him a grandson and had never forgiven me for the fact that my conscience had not allowed me to condone his marriage of some years before.

What could I do? I was helpless before his power. I could only pray that someday I would have the opportunity to help the unfortunate people of my country.

Chapter Twelve

Early in 1922 the Prince of Wales came to Kapurthala at the tail end of a long and strenuous tour; Kapurthala was the last state he visited.

We were charmed by the young heir to the English throne. Handsome and gay, he captivated the state by his lively interest in everything about him. By the time he reached Kapurthala he was exhausted from his weeks of official duties and speeches, but he remained cheerful and smiling throughout his visit.

The maharaja put on an elaborate spectacle for the prince with enormous banquets, entertainment, and fireworks. Since the maharaja's own wives were in purdah, it was up to me to act as hostess.

I was delighted. The prince and I had many friends in common and throughout the long ordeals of lunch and dinner we discussed, like ordinary people, the friends we knew. I was most impressed by the friendliness and democratic spirit of this young man who was later to become king. It seemed to me then that his ease of manner and warmth endeared him to everyone who met him, even on the first encounter.

At the state banquet, it was necessary that he rise to reply to the maharaja's toast of welcome. As the maharaja was saying his last words, the Prince of Wales reached for my hand under the table, smiled wryly, and whispered, "This is always the worst part."

As the Prince of Wales got up to speak, a sudden feeling like a premonition swept over me. Perhaps it was based on the fact that his genial manner seemed too democratic to be that of a king, but as I sat at the table and listened to his talk, I had the strong feeling that he would not rule England. I brushed the thought away as foolishness—how could he not be king? And yet, some accident, death, or illness—I could not visualize what would prevent it. I have thought of that moment many times since his abdication from the British throne—not for death but for love.

Some months after the visit of the Prince of Wales we left India with the maharaja and sailed for Europe. This time the three of us spent more time together than we ever had before. We were in London the spring of that year and the city was buzzing with excitement. The late King George and his bride-to-be, Elizabeth, were soon to be married and one April afternoon we were invited to a party at Buckingham Palace to view the wedding presents. There we met the late Duke of Kent who came over to us, introduced himself, and insisted on showing us all the presents. He was as excited as if it was his own wedding.

London was gayer that year than I had ever known it. For the first time it was more fun to be in England than in France. I was happy to see my old and beloved friend, Lord Hardinge, and we laughed together in remembrance of my career as an "international incident."

The Duke and Duchess of Sutherland entertained us and it was at their lovely home in Green Street that I once again had proof of how small the world is.

As I mingled with the guests while tea was being served I passed by a very beautiful woman who was pouring tea. There was something vaguely familiar about her. She was blonde and elegantly dressed, a typical English beauty.

"Who is she?" I asked Lord Hardinge. "I have the feeling that I know her from somewhere."

Lord Hardinge peered at the woman through his monocle. Then he told me her name. I had never heard it before.

But all afternoon her face nagged at me. It was not only her looks which were familiar; there was something about the way she moved, even about the way she poured the tea which I recognized.

The tea! Of course, *that* was it. I should have recognized her at once. For the elegant woman pouring tea was my little English friend, Sheila, with whom I had played "tea" so many times in Dehra Dun.

I got up from my seat quickly and rushed over to where she was sitting. I introduced myself and we nearly fell into each other's arms. Sheila had grown into a charming woman, not without a sense of humor, for she picked up the teapot and swung it near my face.

"What you deserve now," she laughed, "is for me to take this pot of tea and dump it over *your* head!"

Sheila and I talked for hours about all that had happened to us in the many years since I had last seen her and we were both chagrined at the way we had behaved as children.

"I was a perfect little beast," I confessed, "to have plagued you the way I did."

"It was exactly what I deserved," retorted Sheila, "I was an insufferable prig."

Seeing Sheila had made the years dissolve and for a moment I could remember myself as a child. It is a shock to tear off the veil of age and realize the difference between what you thought life was going to be like and the way it turned out. There is more pain in the remembrance of innocence than there is in disillusionment.

In August of that year we went with the maharaja to Scotland to visit Lord Inchcape at Glenapp Castle, Ayrshire, for grouse-shooting. I had no idea what grouse were but I was game to join in the fun.

The morning of the hunt I arrived punctually in the downstairs hall. In India time means little, but I had learned in Europe that *"l'exactitude c'est la politesse des rois."* But unfortunately I had not yet learned about being correctly dressed for grouse-shooting. When Lord Inchcape saw me in what I thought an infinitely chic, bright red Paris suit, he said, "My dear, you shall frighten the birds away."

I suppose that my cheeks, too, would have frightened away the birds, for they took on the same color as my dress.

Kind Lord Inchcape, however, asked me to follow the hunt on horseback. An enormous horse, as wide as it was long, was brought out of the stable, but the breadth of the horse was too much for me. After riding all day I ached all over and was all the more anxious to get back as I never enjoyed the spectacle of defenseless animals being killed.

The horse's tremendous breadth had another effect on me. Twisting about all day trying to find a more comfortable position had wrought havoc with my lingerie. On our return home as Lord Inchcape helped me to the ground, a tangle of pink silk slipped down my legs and twisted about my dangling feet. Even the staid Britishers standing about had to burst into gales of laughter. I am sure that a British princess would have been able to make a perfect riposte, but I admit that I never felt less a princess than when I bent down, picked it up, and stuffed it into my pocket as though it were a handkerchief.

Shortly after my debacle at Glenapp Castle we returned to Paris before going to India. Paris was at its height of gaiety and there were many changes since the last time we had visited France. Night clubs were swarming with people and for the first time my husband did not object to going about to the night spots.

We escaped one evening from a boring embassy reception with three Americans—reputed to be the three richest men in America (although that was always being said about Americans)—and wandered into an almost unknown little club called the Florence. It was completely deserted except for five Negro musicians who sat disconsolately at their music stand. The waiters stood about in boredom and we were the only guests in the place.

"Let's get out of this dead place," suggested one of the American men.

We got up to leave but when the manager saw himself losing the only business of the night, he motioned to the musicians to start playing. As if they were possessed by a strange magic, the five musicians suddenly sprang to life and played a hot jazz such as I have never heard since. We all sat down again quickly and stayed nearly until dawn listening to the wild excitement of these jazz players.

I could hardly wait to tell my friends. Before the next day had passed I had called almost everyone I knew in Paris and arranged to take them to Le Florence. A few days later we returned with a large party of people; within a week the Florence was crowded nightly with jazz fans. It soon became the most fashionable night club in Paris and remained so for twenty years. After that incident many of my friends teased me by saying they were going to rename the Florence *La Boîte à Brinda*.

Paris society was crowded with gigolos. I could feel nothing but pity for those handsome young men who pushed the old fat women around the dance floor; they more than earned their money. Most of their customers were women of sixty and seventy who covered their faces with rouge and their falling hair with wigs, frantically trying to appear to be in the bloom of youth.

When I was a young girl in Paris, a middle-aged French society woman was content to look her age. All that was changed now in the frenzy of excitement that was sweeping across the world in the twenties. Now there was only one way to look and that way was like a frisky young flapper with coal-scuttle hat, and hair cut straight across the forehead and bunched out at the ears. As I look back I am astonished that I was able to look at myself in the mirror without being horrified by the ugliness of my costumes.

The crazy desperation for gaiety from Paris to Rome, from London to the Riviera, brought out the ugliest aspects of human nature. There was a price for acceptance in this so-called society. Almost everyone was willing to pay it. You could buy a title and its papers then almost as easily as you can buy a tube of toothpaste today. The only difference was that the price was slightly higher.

Counterfeit letters of introduction to famous people, checks forged to pay for gambling debts, and fast motor cars, these were the standards of society of that time. Scandals were bursting like Roman candles all over Europe—only *some* of them were hushed up.

It was not only that people I had known all my life were so hard up for money that they allowed themselves to be mixed up in this sort of intrigue. It was more the story of the times. One could not help but be swept up by the wildness of the twenties.

In June of 1924 the Tika Raja and I, accompanied by the maharaja, were received by the King and Queen of England in Buckingham Palace.

On such an occasion it was necessary that I wear formal Indian dress. I was in a state over which one to wear. At first I chose the brightest and most gaily colored of my saris but Eyres Monsell, who was then chief government whip, advised me that a more subdued sari would be in better taste. I finally chose a black silk chiffon, hand-embroidered with butterflies of gold and silver and colored threads. On my head I wore a headband of diamonds and emeralds, matching emerald-and-diamond drop earrings, and twisted about my neck were three strands of gleaming pearls.

We were received by Their Majesties in a small anteroom. Queen Mary was dressed regally in pale blue and silver with magnificent diamonds. Across her corsage was the blue ribbon of the Garter. Queen Mary smiled cordially at me as I bowed low.

"You were a little uncertain of your English in Delhi some years ago," she said kindly, "but I am told you speak it now as well as you do French."

I was flattered that the queen remembered me so well after all those years. The maharaja did not like the fact that I had been singled out, but King George was kind to me as well and was particularly insistent that I attend the horse show which was scheduled for the following week.

We were conducted by two guards to the ballroom where the maharaja and his son were placed on the dais behind the two thrones. I was given an ornately carved armchair a little to the right where I could see the proceedings clearly.

It was a remarkable occasion in many ways and I was impressed most of all by the efficiency of the English. It was far different from the more careless attitude of Indian royalty. In three hours, more than eight hundred debutantes were presented before the king and queen. The timing and the graciousness of the presentations could not have been better arranged.

Also present on that occasion were the Prince of Wales, the Duke and Duchess of York, the Duke of Connaught, and Prince and Princess Arthus.

When the royal family was ready to leave, a band hidden from sight burst into "God Save the King" and the entire court rose to its feet as the king and queen and their family left at the head of a procession which included all the Indian princes who were present. I walked beside the famous Maharaja of Alwar, who towered above me like a brooding giant. As we passed slowly through the many state rooms lined on both sides with guests, I could overhear whispered remarks which speculated on who I was.

No one had any idea. I was the only Indian woman present and none of the guests realized that I understood English perfectly. It was difficult not to laugh as I walked down the aisle under the barrage of comments.

Some days later the king and queen invited us to lunch with Their Majesties at the horse races at Ascot in the royal box. The road to Ascot was crowded with cars and in the confusion we lost our way. We arrived there three hours late, long after lunch was finished. We tried to be as unobtrusive as possible in the crowd, some distance from the royal box, but Lady Churchill spotted us and insisted that we join her until the race was over.

I was mortified by our inexcusable lateness and felt that our conduct deserved the worst possible punishment. But instead, when the king and queen learned that we had finally arrived, they sent for us and consoled us for having had the bad luck to lose our way. I was overwhelmed by their kindness and it was a great lesson to me to observe the graciousness of those monarchs.

Soon after this we returned to India. It was 1925. Winter in Kapurthala was usually an unhappy time for both my husband and myself. Somehow, there was always trouble of one kind or another.

In the last few years, the maharaja seemed to derive a perverse pleasure from interfering between the Tika Raja and me. This year he was worse than ever.

My marriage had never been a perfect one. But what marriage is? I had grown to accept the problems of our life together and it seemed to me that the Tika Raja had also become more content as the years passed by. He had always been in love with me; in the beginning, perhaps too much so. Not all the fault of our difficulties had been his. As a young girl I had not been ready for the burden of love and this had only accentuated his jealousy and insecurity. But, like many people, in some way he had been able to work out a more satisfactory relationship.

I had grown more fond of my husband as the years passed and at last there was a good deal of understanding and quiet affection between us. But the maharaja seemed determined to make trouble. Possibly, since he disliked me, he could not bear for me to have the affection of his son. Seeing us happy together seemed to infuriate him.

He began to hint to me that all was not well. He pretended to have great sympathy for me. It was almost as if he were consoling me on the failure of my marriage. At first I laughed it off since I could so easily see through his tactics but later it began to upset me.

There are none of us so secure that the constant tearing down of our defenses doesn't have some effect. Gradually, the maharaja's campaign began to work. His constant criticism of me to the Tika Raja also began to work. The result was that we both became irritable and many quarrels resulted. I began to get jittery and my nerves were at a breaking point from the strain.

Just when I was feeling my lowest the maharaja proposed that he and the Tika Raja go off to Europe together for the summer and that I remain in India. The separation, he said, would do our marriage good and he promised that when they returned, all would be well again. By that time I was so exhausted that I no longer cared what happened and I agreed to remain in Kapurthala while they made the trip together.

I took the children to Mussoorie for the hottest months of the year and then returned to our home. In the winter my father's health began to fail. He had never been well after the death of my mother and his exile from Jubbal had made him a broken man.

My late uncle, Rana Padam Chand, had left two sons. The elder son had died at the age of twenty-two so that Bhagat Chand, the younger, now ruled the state. He turned out to be a conscientious ruler and under his development the state's chief source of revenue, the timber forests, increased enormously in value. My father admired his brilliant nephew and also had a good deal of affection for him.

But Bhagat Chand had been brought up to consider my father a villain. He had also been taught that my marriage had brought shame on the Jubbal family and believed that my father had purposely engineered it out of hostility for his relatives.

Still a proud man, my father was reproachful and demanding to his nephew while the raja remained aloof and unforgiving. My father wanted desperately to return to his own state of Jubbal but his nephew would not hear of it. Even when he was an old, sick man, the raja would not allow him to return.

On their last interview my father broke down and wept but it was to no avail.

"Very well," cried my father. "You refuse to honor your father's brother but the day will come when you will take my corpse to the burning ghat!"

This was in the nature of a curse for to carry a body to the funeral pyre is the most painful duty one can perform to the dead.

At the end of the winter, soon after the maharaja and my husband had returned to Kapurthala, we received the news that my father was dying. The maharaja was deeply saddened by the news for they had been lifelong friends. I could not believe it was so and was convinced that with proper care my father would live a long time. I began to prepare a small cottage near our home so that we could send for my father and nurse him back to health. In the meantime I sent my sister Madhvi and my brother Kaju to Simla to be with our father. At home we prepared for the invalid's arrival.

But it was not to be. Just before midnight on the fourteenth of December we received a wire telling us that my father had died at noon that day. The wire explained that he had been conscious to the last and had witnessed all the religious rites which were customary. He had spoken often of his children as he lay dying but the pain of his exile was still uppermost in his mind. His last words, as the breath went out of his body, were "Jubbal! Jubbal!"

My father had always requested that his remains be taken to Hardwar for cremation. It had been many years since I had been in the holy city, but I remembered it well, for it was at that time that the Maharaja of Kapurthala had arranged my marriage to his son. Now I was to return there, not to watch the small paper boats sail in flames down the river, but to bid my father good-by.

My youngest sister, Kamla, and I set out at once by train. A special coach had been attached to the Hardwar-bound train from Simla which connected with our train. We were alone since my husband and the maharaja could not accompany us. Hindu custom says that relatives by marriage cannot have any part in the rites of death. However, the maharaja was grief-stricken and decreed general mourning throughout the state of Kapurthala.

As our train stopped at the dusty station of Hardwar, I saw my cousin Raja Bhagat Chand of Jubbal standing on the platform. I knew that he had not been informed of the death of my father and I wondered what he was doing in Hardwar. Later I found that he had visited the sacred city to perform his annual religious rites at the Ganges.

When he saw our faces as we stepped out of the train he must have had a premonition of what was wrong; he was well aware of the fact that my father was a dying man.

My cousin walked over to me quickly and touched me on the arm.

"What has happened?" he asked anxiously.

I could not meet his eyes. I had little forgiveness in my heart for the man who had refused my father's dying request. I pointed to the funeral car.

"My father is dead," I answered him quietly.

As I spoke, the door of the mortuary car opened and my father's remains were carried out onto the platform. Without another word, the raja stepped forward and motioned one of the bearers aside. Then he put his shoulder to the bier.

Later, as head of the family and ruler of our state he assumed the duties of chief mourner during the last rites. My father's last words had been fulfilled. It was his nephew who carried his body to the banks of the Ganges and placed it on the funeral pyre.

I believe my cousin sincerely regretted that he had not allowed my father to return to Jubbal. After the funeral he tried to effect a reconciliation between our families and in the end I felt I had to forgive him; it was not his fault he had been brought up to feel hostility against us. Eventually relations between our families grew more cordial and the bad, bitter years were nearly forgotten.

Back home in Kapurthala, life seemed easier than it had the months before my father-in-law and husband had made their trip to Europe. The maharaja was amiable and the Tika Raja seemed calmer and more pleasant. My father-in-law assured me that everything was going to be all right.

I was relieved. My last ordeal of the death of my father had exhausted me and I was weary from sorrow. I rested and tried to find some comfort in the fact that things were going well.

I did not know it was the calm before the storm.

Chapter Thirteen

Ever since the birth of my youngest daughter I had been trying to conceive another child in order to present my husband with a longed-for heir. But our efforts were in vain. The fault probably lay in the fact that childbirth in India is not scientific and that the relatively primitive delivery of my babies had done enough harm to prevent another conception.

Several times I had consulted European doctors but the verdict was always the same. In order to have another child it would be necessary for me to have a series of treatments to repair the damage which had been done. Since my husband was reconciled to the fact that we had no sons and since there was no guarantee that if I did conceive once more it would be a boy, I hesitated to undergo the long and painful treatments which would have been necessary.

But my father-in-law had his own ideas on this matter.

Shortly after my father's death, my husband came to me and said that the maharaja requested my presence in an important conference among the three of us. One look at the Tika Raja's face and I knew that something out of the ordinary had happened. When I asked my husband what was wrong, he refused to tell me and acted so queerly that I became apprehensive. Later I realized that he was embarrassed by what was about to take place.

We met in the maharaja's study. He motioned us to sit down and began speaking at once. He had no trace of embarrassment.

"Brinda," he began in a matter-of-fact voice, "you undoubtedly realize the disappointment you have caused my son and myself by not producing an heir."

I nodded my head but did not answer. My brain spun with what he was saying. What was behind all this? I thought.

The maharaja looked at me coldly. His face was hard with determination.

"It is necessary that you have a son," he said.

"I am perfectly willing," I answered quickly, "but it does not seem to be possible."

The maharaja fingered some papers on his desk.

"I understand," he said, "that some treatments would be necessary . . ."

I looked at my husband who twisted about nervously in his chair. He looked away and would not meet my eyes.

"The Tika Raja and I have discussed such a measure," I said. "It is painful and somewhat dangerous. We decided not to go ahead with it."

My father-in-law looked at his son who now stared out the window in an effort not to be drawn into our conversation.

"My son has changed his mind," the maharaja replied.

"Then why didn't he tell me about it?" I asked hotly.

"I am telling you for him," he replied. "He is in complete agreement with everything I am saying."

I turned to the Tika Raja accusingly.

"Is that so?" I asked him.

The Tika Raja looked shamefaced. Once more he avoided meeting my eyes. For a moment he did not answer.

"Your wife has asked you a question," the maharaja said firmly. "Answer her."

"Yes," mumbled my husband. "My father is right."

"I am willing," the maharaja continued, "to pay for all the expenses of the treatment. My only condition is that they be started as soon as possible. It is of utmost importance that an heir be brought into the state of Kapurthala."

"You know that the treatments must be done in Europe?" I asked.

"You may leave at once," answered my father-in-law. "Every cooperation will be given you. On my part, I will do everything I can to help. We have not been friends in the past, my dear, but I promise you that when you bear a son, all will be different."

There was nothing more for me to say. It was clear enough that both my husband and father-in-law believed that it was my duty to produce a son at any cost. Perhaps they were right. I agreed to go through the treatments even though I was well aware of the pain and illness involved.

My father-in-law seemed pleased at my acquiescence and my husband acted as though he were relieved that no harsh words had resulted from the interview. I got up from my chair to go. But the maharaja put out his hand and waved me back to my seat.

"There is something more I want to tell you," he said.

Now my husband looked as if he wanted to disappear from the room. I was puzzled. What more could there be?"

The maharaja cleared his throat.

"In the event that you do *not* produce an heir," he said, "it will be necessary for the Tika Raja to take another wife."

The blood rushed to my head. I felt faint with anger. Would the maharaja humiliate me to that extent?

"I would never agree to such a thing," I cried.

The maharaja's voice was icy. "You would have no choice," he said. "It is perfectly proper for my son to take another wife if he so chooses."

"But he would not do that to me," I answered, close to tears.

The Tika Raja looked away. I could tell by the expression on his face that he would do whatever his father demanded. I knew, too, that the matter had been discussed before our meeting and that my husband was in agreement with this barbaric plan.

My anger left me. There was no point to wreaking fury on either my father-in-law or my husband. For the Tika Raja I could feel only contempt for his weakness; my father-in-law I despised with all my heart. In that moment,

I lost any remaining respect for my husband. I felt pity for his weakness but little sympathy for his lack of courage.

Without another word, I got up from my chair and left the room. I had agreed to go through with the treatments and I was willing to keep my word. But it was with a heavy heart that I went back to my home and began preparations to return to Europe.

Once more on the boat, as I sat on the deck chair watching the gray sea tumble before my eyes, I tried to find comfort in the words of the Gita. If only I could truly give up my desires and learn to live apart from the world, then maybe I would find happiness.

> Not shaken by adversity
> Not hankering after happiness
> Free from fear, free from anger
> Free from the things of desire.

I longed to be able to renounce my flesh and retreat from the world but I still was not able to do it.

While I was reading, I came across a remarkable paragraph. It seemed to have been written for me:

> If you desire the world and know at the same time that such desires are regarded as wicked, you, perhaps, will not dare to plunge into the struggle. Yet your mind will be running day and night with desire. This is hypocrisy and will serve no purpose. Plunge into the world, and then, after a time, when you have suffered and enjoyed all that is in it, renunciation will come; calmness will come. So fulfil your desire for power and everything else and after you have fulfilled the desire, will come the time when you

will know that they are all very little things. But until you have fulfilled this desire, until you have passed through that activity, it is impossible for you to come to the state of calmness, serenity, and self-surrender.

I let the book fall on my lap. Its wisdom was irrefutable. There was no way I could achieve peace of mind by reading about it. Obviously I was not ready to give up the delights of the world. Maybe my suffering would teach me the calmness I yearned after. Until then I could only throw myself into the world of pleasures and pain.

And the place to do it was surely Europe at the end of the twenties. For never again did pleasure sprawl over a continent as it did then across the pale sands of the Riviera and the noisy, smoke-filled bistros of Paris.

My husband and I stayed at the Ritz in Paris. Since I expected to spend quite a bit of time in France for my treatments, I began to look out for a small apartment.

There were more parties in Paris than ever. Added to the regular rounds of entertainment there was a new kind of party in operation. Those were the ones engineered by Elsa Maxwell. Armed with a remarkable personality and an enormous zest for living, she was the answer to many a poor millionaire's prayer.

Overnight a millionaire could become the most popular man in Paris. All he had to do was contact Elsa and arrange a few small parties (several-hundred guests) or sometimes he could sit back and wait until Elsa contacted him. Good businesswoman that she was, she knew which millionaires needed helping.

I don't think she ever engineered a party that wasn't a

success. She claimed she had only one rule—"Never ask two kings to the same party."

Cole Porter was another American of whom I grew fond. He and his wife entertained lavishly and we saw a good deal of them both. With his tip-tilted nose and tiny stature he was like an enchanting Pied Piper—guests clamored to hear his songs as he sat at the piano.

He had a wonderful sense of humor, too. One night as I sat next to him in a jazz night club in Paris, he looked around the smoke-filled room at couples wildly dancing about, shouting and laughing, turned to me and said, "They're all trying so hard to be gay. It's as if they're saying to themselves, 'Let's misbehave!' "

I laughed so uproariously at the picture of these grown people *trying* to be naughty that he was enchanted. He told me that he was writing a song and would use that as its title.

"What's more, Brinda," he said, "I'm going to autograph 'Let's Misbehave' for you."

I was delighted when it became a hit nearly overnight.

I spent a week aboard Lord Inchcape's yacht. His daughter, Elsie MacKay, was a close friend of mine. One afternoon all of us were invited to tea on Marconi's yacht, *Electra,* by Prince Potenziani who later became governor of Rome. I was thrilled to meet the inventor of the wireless and he was kind enough to show me his research room where scattered about were wires, electrical equipment, and all sorts of magical-looking odds and ends. Marconi, a serious-faced man with deep-set eyes, was not very talkative but he was vastly amused when I pointed to the array of equipment in his laboratory and said, "If only some of the Indian fakirs who hang about the market place could get hold of your equipment. What magic they could make out of it!"

In August I went to Venice alone. My relations with the Tika Raja were considerably cooler since our interview in Kapurthala with his father. We were still friends but I had lost any remaining faith in him.

I was willing to go ahead with the treatments and planned to return to Paris soon to begin the necessary consultations. But my husband and I agreed that although on the surface things would remain much the same, actually it would be better for both of us if we were freer to lead our own lives.

I spent only a few days in Venice that summer as I had agreed to accompany some friends on a motor tour to Amalfi, Sorrento, and Naples. The last of our trip was at Capri where we spent an unforgettable week.

We sailed in boats in the Blue Grotto where we saw the inkiness of the water turn to a clear and radiant blue before our eyes, we stretched out on the pointed rocks and watched the incredible sapphire of the Mediterranean sparkle under the glinting Italian sun, we drank small cups of bitter black coffee and gossiped about the people we knew who walked by.

We danced on terraces in the shadows under a golden crescent nearly hidden by clouds; we bargained in the small shops and wore silly straw hats on our heads and flimsy mules on our feet. We even visited the ruins of Tiberius' castle on the edge of a cliff. Tiberius had made

Capri famous as a pleasure island in the times of the Roman emperors. My favorite story about him was that when he was displeased with a week-end guest, he would call him to the edge of the terrace and then several guards would push the guest off the cliff onto the sharp rocks below. Privately I thought that I had known some guests who would merit the same treatment.

One afternoon while I was basking in the hot sun a handsome young American came over to our group. He knew several of my friends but since I was lying on a rock we were not introduced. Several minutes after his arrival, however, he came over to me.

"I've been watching you all day," he said. "May I sit here with you?"

I sat up on my rock and squinted at him.

"If you like," I answered.

Promptly he sat down and settled himself next to me. He introduced himself and then looked at me questioningly.

I realized that he had no idea who I was, and I felt delighted and relieved to be just a woman for a change instead of a princess. I looked at him demurely.

"My name is Brinda," I said.

"That's a lovely name," he said with a sigh. I nearly giggled out loud. It wasn't really funny but he seemed so infatuated. I thought it wicked of me to allow him to flirt with me but I was flattered, too. Nothing restores a woman's ego like that sort of attention from a man, because he did not seem capricious but genuinely smitten.

We talked all afternoon about the places we had been

and the people we had known but mostly about how nice it was to be sitting in the sun at Capri. I was amused by him and particularly by his attitude towards me. He thought I was a helpless girl, alone, who needed his protection.

As the day wore on I felt guilty about my pose but by now I was too embarrassed to confess. However, as the sun slipped down behind the cliffs and it was time to leave the beach, the young man seized my hand and begged to know if he could see me that evening.

Our flirtation had gone far enough. I told him I was busy and that it would be impossible for me to see him again.

"I must see you again," he cried. "I don't even know your name."

I slipped into my mules, picked up my towel, and stepped down from the rock. Then I turned to say good-by.

"I am Princess Brinda of Kapurthala," I said, "and it was not fair of me to tease you. I'm sorry and I do beg your pardon."

The young man's face dropped in astonishment. Then he grinned and shook my hand heartily.

"I *shall* see you tonight, after all," he laughed. "I have been invited specially to meet you by our friends."

That evening as we danced together on the terrace of a villa which jutted out over the shining sea the young American told me that he had fallen deeply in love with me at first sight and wanted to marry me.

I tried to be as kind as possible because he was pale with seriousness.

"Such a thing would be impossible," I said gently. "I am

already married. My husband is heir to the throne of Kapurthala."

The young American was a good sport and took the news well. We agreed to remain friends and he did not reproach me for the trick which I had played on him.

When I returned to Paris I began a series of painful treatments in the hope that I could bear my husband an heir. For the first time I enjoyed being alone and spent my days reading, visiting museums, and resting in the quiet of my small apartment. I had had enough of people for a while. It was good to be away from the frenetic gaiety.

Sometimes I went to the Duchess de la Rochefoucauld's home where each Wednesday she collected the literary and artistic talent of Paris. It was the nearest thing to a *salon* in the postwar years. Although my formal education had been far from thorough, I enjoyed meeting these exciting artists and it was a relief to hear something discussed besides society gossip.

After the course of treatment was completed I made arrangements to return to India. When I arrived Kapurthala seemed peaceful and I prayed that things would go well there this time. But it was not destined to be so.

At first the maharaja seemed glad to see me. My husband was delighted that the course of treatment was over and that there was hope that we would have an heir. For the first few weeks everything went smoothly.

But after months passed I could see there was trouble brewing. So far, there was no reason to believe that the treatments had been successful. The strain of what I had undergone in Paris and the ordeal of having to remain in Kapurthala, which I sensed was a growingly hostile environment, was exhausting me.

As time went on my father-in-law grew more and more discontented that we had no news for him. He took his irritation out on me, and used every excuse to provoke a quarrel. He told me that he was opposed to my returning to Europe and that he was sick of my way of life.

In spite of the fact that he had spent most of his own years traveling around the world and that he had robbed me of any chance of making a life for my husband and myself in Kapurthala, he insisted that I remain at home. Then he had the audacity to accuse me of neglecting my children.

He knew when he said this how it would wound me for I loved my children dearly and during the winter months which I always spent in India the little girls were with me constantly. Far from neglecting them, I came dangerously close to monopolizing them. During the summer the children went to their grandfather's place in Mussoorie with three governesses, one French and two English. They had little time for me in the summer and my trips to Europe had done them no harm at all. The maharaja, however, insisted that it was my duty to accompany them to Mussoorie each year. He claimed that my failure to do so had become a scandal throughout India.

We both knew this was untrue but there was no way I could refute it. All I could do was to try to go on as best I could under the pressures of these false accusations.

He further accused me of flouting his authority by leaving India without his permission and claimed I was causing additional scandal by traveling about Europe alone. I told him that I was willing to seek formal permission before leaving India and also that I would be delighted to have a suitable woman companion.

But all this was beside the point. The maharaja knew that I had always behaved with the utmost propriety; this new attack on me was only a way of undermining me once again in order to prove that I was a failure not only because I had not produced a son but in everything else as well.

I became more nervous every day. I saw quite a bit of the Tika Raja and naturally it was a strain for both of us. He was intimidated by his father and was afraid to stand up for either himself or me and I could not have much respect for him because of his fear. In Europe we had agreed to more or less live separately; now we were forced into an intimacy that was neither welcome nor familiar.

By the end of the winter it was more or less apparent that the treatments had been unsuccessful. I was feeling depressed and tired and wept at the slightest provocation. Days went by where I spent my time sitting in a darkened room or reading in a chair by the window. I had no desire to see anyone and the thought of official dinners or parties threw me into a panic. After a while I refused to accept callers and stayed alone most of the time.

The Tika Raja became quite concerned over the change in me. I had always been cheerful and hopeful; now suddenly I had changed into a morbidly hopeless woman. I felt stranded and alone; there seemed to be nothing that could comfort me.

Finally I felt that I could bear it no longer. Even I became worried about my condition and my apathy. I knew that somehow I had to pull myself together but it did not seem possible under the conditions of life in Kapurthala. Then I thought that perhaps if I returned to Europe I would feel better again. The exhausting treatments and the unfriendly atmosphere of Kapurthala had worn me out. I decided that I would ask the maharaja for permission to visit Europe for the summer in an effort to regain my health.

But he was furious at my request and sent me a message saying in no uncertain terms that it had been refused. I knew that it was necessary that I leave India so I asked my husband to intercede for me. He spoke to his father and pleaded with him to allow me to leave but the maharaja was adamant. He was determined that I remain in India until I produced an heir.

By this time I was desperate. I was feeling more nervous and panicky each day and was worried that soon I would break down completely. It seemed that no one was going to help me. I would have to help myself.

I sent the maharaja a note saying that I regretted that he was unable to give me permission to leave India but that my situation was desperate and that I had made arrangements to depart the following month.

The maharaja was furious at what he termed my wilful disobedience of his orders and commanded my husband to stop my allowance at once. The Tika Raja, however, stood his ground firmly this time and refused to do so.

So angry was my father-in-law, however, that he immediately contacted the Punjab government and tried to persuade them to hold up my passport. He was further incensed when he received an official denial of his request. The Tika Rani, they said, was not a political prisoner. The government could not prevent her from leaving India.

My husband was worried about me and suggested that we travel to Europe together. However, he told me that his father would be on the same boat and I decided that in my state of mind it would be better if I traveled alone.

I arranged to leave on the same boat with Lady Birdwood and her son, Christopher, the present Lord Birdwood, and we sailed from Karachi early in April. I did not look forward to the trip. I only hoped that I would feel some peace.

Chapter Fourteen

The first thing I did when I arrived in Paris was to make an appointment with the doctor who had given me the treatments the previous year. After a thorough check-up he gave me his verdict. The treatments had failed. Unless I underwent a major operation, I would never be able to have another child.

The news was a terrible blow to me for all during the painful year past I believed that the result would be to bear another child. Now the doctor also made it clear that the operation was a dangerous one and that I would be running considerable risk to have it performed. He advised against it.

Disturbed by the consultation, I wired my husband who was visiting with his father in the south of France and he joined me at once in Paris. Neither of us pretended any longer that there was any love between us but the Tika

Raja felt much affection for me and at this time was full of kindness and concern for my well-being.

He discussed my condition with the doctor and came to see me in my small apartment. He seemed worried.

"I will never consent," he declared, "to your risking your life."

"There is no other way I can bear a child," I answered.

The Tika Raja was greatly agitated. He walked up and down the room for a bit in indecision. Finally he sat down heavily.

"Then you will not bear an heir," he said.

I waited a moment before speaking and tried to think through carefully what I was about to say. Much depended on it.

"Since I am not willing to accept the consequences of not bringing a son into the world," I said quietly, "there is no alternative."

The Tika Raja looked embarrassed. He was well aware of my feelings about his father's threat of my husband's remarriage.

"It is more important," he said, "that we consider your health."

"Under the circumstances," I answered, "I think it only fair that the decision be left up to me."

After the Tika Raja left I spent many hours trying to decide whether or not to have the operation. In the end I felt it was the only thing to do. I was touched by my husband's solicitous attitude but I was still afraid of my father-in-law's wrath. I called the doctor and told him that I had decided to go through with the operation.

The next day I had a long talk with the doctor. He told me that I was in no condition to undergo such an operation immediately and refused to accept the responsibility of this drastic measure until my general health improved. He advised me to leave Paris so that I build up my resistance.

I called the Tika Raja and he agreed that waiting a few months would be wise although he still maintained that he preferred I did not take the risk of the operation at all.

During these preparations my father-in-law arrived in Paris. We were no longer speaking to each other so I did not see him but tales about him followed me everywhere. Once again he was trying to make life difficult for me. He told everyone that I was a wicked woman who delighted in aggravating him and he complained of my bad conduct in visiting Europe without his permission. But he got little sympathy from my friends who were delighted that I was with them again.

In London the maharaja even went to the extent of asking the India Office to remove my name from the list of those invited to official functions. But here he was sharply rebuffed. My friends refused to listen to him and every kindness was shown me by both the India Office and the king and queen of England.

Before leaving Paris I visited the Duchess de la Rochefoucauld at the Chateau de Montmiraille where the family has lived for centuries. The guest of honor at lunch was the late King Fuad of Egypt, an affable man, clever (some people called him crafty), and well informed.

I was startled when I first met him by the strange, hoarse bark which preceded his every remark, a curious, strangling sound from the back of his throat. I wondered if he had been born with this odd speech impediment; later I learned it was the result of an attempted assassination on his life when he was still a young man. It was a miracle he had escaped at all with his life. A bullet had pierced his throat and had caused this weird bark which remained with him for the rest of his life.

One morning while I was sitting near a window in my apartment, drinking a cup of tea, there was a knock on the door. I answered it and for a moment could hardly believe my eyes. It was my old governess, Mlle Meillon. We had not seen each other since I was a young girl; she embraced me and spent the day recalling my early life in India and our trip to France together. Mlle Meillon had found out from friends where I was staying and had come to see me at once. It was in the nature of a farewell visit, for Mlle Meillon was leaving for South America. As a matter of fact it was the last time we were to see each other.

The doctor had recommended that I visit some seaside place to recuperate and I finally decided on Venice. Instead of staying on the noisy and tourist-frequented Lido, I took an apartment consisting of a whole floor in Count and Countess Sangro's *palazzo*. I spent my days resting in the cool terrace and visiting the churches and galleries in Venice. I hired a motor launch for my stay and was able to get around the canals and go back and forth to the Lido.

The Lido was as crowded as ever with my old friends and it was hard to refrain from seeing them. But I was far from well and determined to regain my health so I lived as quietly as possible.

The social event of the season, and one even I could not

miss, was the arrival of the crown prince of Italy. I learned about his visit from Prince Phillip of Hesse while we were watching a regatta. Prince Phillip was no longer the exile of 1920. He had become a person of importance once again. He was now married to a daughter of the king of Italy, Princess Mafalda.

The day following the arrival of Crown Prince Umberto, a fiesta was held in his honor. The famous flyer, Colonel Ferrarini, had promised to fly me over Venice and the beach that day as I had never seen Venice from the air.

I peered out at the winding canals and long strip of beach from the air and I felt safe and confident in the capable hands of Colonel Ferrarini. But suddenly, as we were directly over the Lido, the colonel began to put the plane through a series of acrobatics. I was strapped to my seat but I had had no warning of what was about to happen and as the plane looped, rolled, banked, and dived, I screamed in terror. All I could do was hold onto my seat and pray.

When the plane landed I staggered out onto the ground, my head and stomach still reeling from the stunts. This was no way to recover my health! As soon as I could get my breath, I turned to the colonel and scolded him for the ordeal.

He shrugged his shoulders.

"I could not help it," he said. "I was signaled from the ground to perform my stunts for the entertainment of the crown prince. I am sorry you did not like it."

Did not like it? I shook my head in dismay. I had nearly been frightened to death.

The colonel laughed at my fears.

"What you need is a champagne cocktail," he said, leading me into the Lido bar. "That is good for the nerves."

Just as we sat down, we were summoned to the crown prince who wanted to congratulate the colonel. When Prince Umberto saw me he was horrified. He had had no idea that Ferrarini had a passenger; knowing his skill as a stunt flier, he had asked for the display but did not know I would have to share the honor.

"You're a plucky woman," said the prince and taking me by the hand he led both the colonel and myself onto the terrace. He signaled the crowd below that we had been in the plane together as it careened through the air and the thousands of people below cheered us loudly. I felt that I did not deserve any applause. I had been anything but a willing victim.

The next day, after a luncheon party given on the beach by Countess Frasso, the prince took me to watch the motorboat races. The main event was a contest between the English ace, Seagrave, and an American named Gar Wood. But in the middle of the race there was a bad collision and Prince Umberto left immediately for the hospital. Luckily the injuries had been minor although I was convinced at the time of the collision that they had both been killed.

After a ball that night at the Countess Morosini's Prince Umberto left Venice. I saw him off but it was only the first of many times we were destined to meet in our lives.

In the many years I had spent visiting Europe I had heard much about America. All my friends had tried to persuade me for a long time to visit this relatively new and wonderful country. Since I still had to wait before going ahead with my operation in Paris, my friends insisted that I accompany them to America, at least for a few weeks.

It was something I had always wanted to do. So I returned to Paris, packed my things, and left on the French liner *Paris* from Le Havre.

The crossing on the North Atlantic was rough and I spent the entire voyage in bed. But I was rewarded for my trip by the sight of the sky line of New York as we slid up the harbor in the dusk of the evening. The pointed buildings towering into the sky looked like a fairyland perched on a cloud. No castles or palaces I had ever seen before seemed to have such a magic quality as New York with the mist swirled about the buildings dotted with lights.

My American friends were happy to show me their country. It was strange and wonderful to see such remarkable progress. How different from India! In New York, people bustled about their work—they seemed to know where they were going, and in comparison to the poverty of India, everyone looked so prosperous and healthy.

It was 1929 and there was prohibition. But I discovered this meant only that people drank more than ever before. I saw my first football game and here I was frankly horrified to learn that almost every spectator had a hip flask with him and that a large number of them were drunk before the game was half over. Prohibition seemed hardly the way to stop drinking in America.

I had been in America a short time when the great crash of Wall Street happened. Overnight it seemed that all of New York was bankrupt. Many people I had known for years in Europe as millionaires were now penniless.

All my acquaintances seemed stricken by the crash; it was like living in the midst of a frightful epidemic. No one knew at which moment he would succumb. It was embarrassing to go anywhere at that time for it was not always possible to tell who had been affected. Nevertheless, many people tried to carry on as though nothing had happened. Others were not so brave. I had met some in Europe who later leapt from their windows in despair.

I ran into Condé Nast, the publisher, quite by chance. When I had met him in Europe the previous year he promised that if I ever came to New York he would give me a party to remember. He reminded me of that promise when I saw him. At first I demurred but he insisted although he was leaving for Europe on business the following day. He began telephoning immediately and in a couple of hours had invited over eighty people to a party he gave in my honor.

I had planned to stay in America only a short time and before I knew it my visit was over. I had scarcely had time to look around the vast country when I was back on a boat, this time the *Olympic*. I couldn't help thinking when I went into my stateroom and saw it crowded with flowers, champagne, fruit, and books, that under the circumstances of the crash it was wasteful luxury, but it was typical of the generous American hospitality which I had seen over and again on my visit.

In Europe the talk was all of the financial debacle in America and everyone was anxious to learn my first-hand impressions of the crash.

I also found on my return to Paris that rumors had been

flying about me. There was speculation as to why the Tika Raja and I seldom went anywhere together. There was talk that we would divorce. My intimate friends knew the truth: I was trying to give my husband an heir and also that for a Hindu couple such as we there could be no question of divorce.

My husband's family did not help matters. There are always those who are willing to gossip and even more who are willing to listen. My in-laws seemed to take a perverse delight in spreading the rumor that I was about to be repudiated by my husband, not only because I was unable to give him an heir but also because of my conduct in Europe. There was nothing I could do about such slander. It was obvious that they were currying favor with the maharaja and he was no doubt delighted by their attitude.

My friends were alarmed at the stories but I was past caring. There is a point beyond which you can no longer be hurt.

In August I went down to Biarritz with friends. One day we drove across the Spanish border to San Sebastian where we had arranged to see a bullfight. The pageantry of the crowds, the music, and the colorful matador were exciting but I was horrified by the bullfight. To me it was no sport but a cruel and barbaric practice. In fact, I was so horrified that I still remembered it vividly a few years later when I met King Alphonso XIII of Spain in Biarritz. When His Majesty asked me how I had liked his country I told him that I had only been to San Sebastian, but that the gory spectacle of the bullfight still haunted me.

I asked him why he didn't have bullfighting stopped.

The King of Spain looked at me with a cryptic smile and said, "Would you rather see *my* head cut off?"

After the bullfight we drove back to Biarritz and shortly thereafter I returned to Paris for my operation. The doctor assured me that my health had improved and that there was no longer much risk.

On the day of the operation the Tika Raja, my sister Madhvi, and my old friend Beatrix waited at the hospital for hours while I was in the operating room. I saw them for a moment just after I came out of the anesthetic.

I was seriously ill for weeks afterward. Later it took many more weeks of convalescence to make me well again but the time passed and before too long I was back in my own little apartment again.

As soon as I was well enough I sailed for India but I was far from strong and spent most of that voyage in bed, too. A week after we were out to sea I received a radiogram from my dear friend Beatrix telling me of the death of her sixteen-year-old son. I was immeasurably shocked at her tragedy for Beatrix was as dear to me as if she had been my own sister. It was with her that I had known the joys and sorrows of growing up.

I left Bombay on the afternoon of my arrival and hurried straight to Kapurthala. There was much to be done there. My three girls were now growing up. I had to supervise their education and see that they had the proper instruction.

My eldest daughter, Indira, was home on vacation. She had been a boarder at Queen Mary's College for Girls at Lahore. In the beginning, she had fought against the idea of going away to school but now Indira seemed happy there and it had taught her that there was another world outside our palace. In spite of the fact that my children's upbringing had been far more modern and simpler than mine, still they were being raised as princesses and Indira had come dangerously close to being spoiled. Several months of contact with other girls, however, had done wonders for her. Now, she announced, she wanted to work and become an actress at the first opportunity.

By the spring of 1932 I was feeling well again. At that time, my old friend, Indira of Baroda, by then the Maharani of Cooch-Behar, invited me to a tiger shoot she had arranged in honor of her nephew, the heir to Baroda. Indira, at that time, was acting as regent for her son after the death of her husband, and I was astonished to see the changes and improvements she had made in her state. The whole area, and the city, had been modernized. With a pang of envy I realized Indira had done with Cooch-Behar what I had longed to see accomplished in Kapurthala. She had performed a remarkable job and it proved how much could be done for the people of India.

On the day of the tiger shoot we left the palace at eight o'clock in the morning. The sun was already hot in the sky and the day was clear. We had to travel thirty miles by car in order to get close to the jungle.

When we arrived at the edge of the jungle there were more than twenty-five elephants waiting for us. We mounted the elephants. There were seats for four on each elephant but only two of us went on each beast. When everyone was settled the giant animals moved slowly into the jungle for about three miles.

Then the men brought out the tigers. As each tiger came out of the jungle, he looked around, leaped toward the elephants, and the hunters aimed and fired. One of the dangers in such hunting is that if a tiger is wounded and goes back into the jungle he will kill on sight. There is some danger to the elephants as well, for the tigers often attack them. But elephants are trained to take care of themselves before these animals. They defend themselves with their trunks, throw the tiger down on the ground, and step on him. However, if an elephant has been badly trained, there is danger to the person mounted on him for tigers have been known to climb on such an elephant and drag someone off his back.

But our tiger shoot was a great success without mishap. It was very exciting to be mounted on the elephant and I scarcely dared breathe as the row of beasts advanced deeper into the heart of the damp, hot jungle. As the elephants walked I could hear the thousands of tiny animals and birds screeching among the trees and lush foliage.

I saw two tigers that day, three bears, two leopards, and many wild boar and hyenas. The *Yuvraj* of Baroda shot one of the tigers and an American shot the other, but most of the other animals escaped. As a joke they photographed me with one foot on a dead tiger. Whenever I wanted to prove how brave I was after that, I would take out my photograph and show that I was a fine *shikari* (hunter).

Although I do not like to witness the slaughter of animals, I admit that tiger hunting with the Maharani of Cooch-Behar was exciting! At least the tigers had equal chances of either escaping or of killing their opponents and, in a way, it was a contest of skill between man and beast.

Some maharajas actually shoot tigers from the top of stone towers. Sitting there in comfortable armchairs, the hunters await the arrival of an exhausted and frightened tiger whom several hundred beaters, spread in a circle, push to the foot of the tower. Then a hunter shoots at this perfectly exposed target. If by chance he misses there always is an expert nearby who fires the final shot.

I think the loveliest idea is that of the Maharaja Rana of Dholphur, an orthodox Hindu, who invited us to a night tiger hunt. Mounted on elephants, we went deep into the jungle to a huge tree on which was constructed a carefully concealed platform. We climbed a rope ladder and installed ourselves on the platform. It was a dark night and I saw almost nothing until enormous spotlights, high in a tree, were turned on a few hundred feet from us. The night was lit as though a full moon had suddenly come through the clouds! In front of us was a huge clearing next to a lake. Tied to one of the few trees still standing was a goat, used as bait, bleating piercingly. Other than that there was no sound. We remained silent and almost completely motionless for over an hour. Then suddenly, as though from nowhere, came the first tiger. Three more swiftly followed. They moved up slowly and cautiously, drank from the lake, flicked their tails nervously and looked in all directions. Though the goat could not see the tigers, it sensed their presence and bleated louder than ever. But the tigers took no notice of the goat, and moved around with so much grace and rhythm that I was completely enchanted.

After what seemed to me a very long time, one of the tigers suddenly bounded toward the goat, then leaped high in the air for the kill. At that instant a terrifying noise came from the brush where the hundreds of beaters were concealed. The tigers fled instantly into the jungle, the unharmed goat was untied and taken back. It was the end of the tiger hunt and, to me, the most humane and lovely way of enjoying those royal cats.

I found much unhappiness at the palace of Kapurthala when I returned. My brother-in-law, Mahijit Singh, was dangerously ill. I visited him daily but there was no hope for Mahijit; the doctors had pronounced his illness fatal. I was very sad over this news and since I was leaving early in April to return as usual to France, I went to say good-by to him.

He seemed to know that it was our last meeting. His face was drawn and thin and his hand, when he clasped mine, had lost its strength. When he spoke he had tears in his eyes.

"I have been lying here for weeks now and I have had much time to think. Kapurthala is doomed if someone does not save it. There is only you, sister. You must do what you can."

Although I knew that Mahijit was dying I could not pretend.

"What can I do?" I asked. "The maharaja will listen to

no one, least of all to me. He hates me and so do all the family."

"We do not hate you," he answered gently, "although we have treated you badly. It has all come from stupid jealousy. But you must promise to save Kapurthala. You are the only one who can do it. The government is corrupt and my brother is weak."

My brother-in-law looked at me pleadingly. "You must promise me before I die," he said.

"I promise," I said solemnly. "But you realize," I added, "that I can only try. In the past I have begged your father to listen to his children but he has always refused. I will go on trying but that is all I can do."

We were both in tears when I finally left. It was a tragedy that he was dying. Apart from my personal feelings, he was the most gifted of the maharaja's sons and though only thirty-six he was minister of education in the United Provinces. He could have done great things for Kapurthala.

That evening I left for Bombay and my boat sailed for France two days later. We were out to sea only two hours when I received a radiogram announcing that my brother-in-law, Mahijit, was dead.

Chapter Fifteen

I observed the traditional Hindu mourning period of thirteen days on the ship and remained in solitude except for occasional visits in my stateroom from the Maharaja of Rajpipla and the Begum of Mamdot.

The first month in Paris was a dreary one. I had too much on my mind to enjoy the frivolity of France; I preferred to be alone.

My health was not good at that time and I spent my days convalescing in my small apartment. Occasionally, I received callers and my favorite one turned out to be the exiled King Alfonso of Spain. I had known his beautiful Queen Victoria Eugenia in London and was delighted when he sent an envoy to my apartment asking if he might call on me.

We spent an interesting afternoon together. Although we were two strangers we talked intimately and I felt as if

I had known him all my life. Sometimes two people on first acquaintance are able to understand more about each other than friends of long standing. It was that way with us.

The king was still deeply shocked over his exile from Spain the previous year. He was convinced, however, that he would someday return. Having heard of my interest in horoscopes he half-jokingly asked me to get his cast and let him know the result. I promised. But some weeks later when I had received an answer from India I broke my word. I could not bear to tell the king that his ambition would never be fulfilled.

I saw the doctor once again who had performed the operation on me. I told him that I still had not conceived a child after nearly a year in India and he examined me carefully. When he was through he motioned me into his office.

I was stunned by his diagnosis. The operation had been to no avail. In his opinion I would be unable to bear another child.

I felt that it was my duty to tell my husband this news and I wrote him a letter at once. As soon as he arrived in Paris, some weeks later, he came to my apartment.

He was in a state of agitation and as soon as I saw him I knew that something had happened. He was barely inside the door when he began to speak.

"Brinda," he said, "I don't quite know how to begin."

I dreaded to hear his news for I still was not well and felt that I had all the trouble I could bear for the moment. But no matter how I felt I had to face the facts. I waited for the Tika Raja to continue.

"I have told my father," he continued, "that your operation was unsuccessful."

"Oh?" I asked, apprehensive of what was to follow. "How did he take the news?"

"You must know without asking," said the Tika Raja. "He insists that I return to India and take a second wife."

I had expected this blow for many months now but it did not soften the effect for me.

"What do you intend to do?" I asked wearily.

The Tika Raja looked distraught. His hands trembled and he seemed helpless.

"I must return to India at once," he replied, not meeting my eyes, "but I shall protest against this attempt to force me into a second marriage."

I sighed. I knew only too well the limitations of my husband's character. His intentions toward me were fine but his ability to resist the demands of his father was almost nonexistent.

"Why pretend any longer?" I asked him, sick to death of the masquerade. "You know perfectly well you will do whatever your father tells you."

The Tika Raja seized my hands almost in desperation.

"You must believe me, Brinda," he cried, "I shall never let him do this dreadful thing to you. I assure you that I will not take a second wife."

Now I was angry. All my exhaustion from the arduous treatments and the months of nervous strain had suddenly piled up. I wanted to be quiet but the words tumbled out.

"Your father is a strong man," I retorted, "and you are less than nothing in his hands. You have always done exactly what he wanted you to do. You will not stop now."

The Tika Raja was nearly in tears. Over and over again he pleaded with me to believe in him and have faith that he could resist his father. To soothe him, I promised, but they were empty words. After many years I knew my husband too well.

Soon after our interview my husband sailed for India. I was disheartened but not surprised when I received a wire from him six weeks later.

"The worst has happened—I was forced to marry against my will."

In January, 1933, I returned to Kapurthala. My three girls welcomed me home with more eagerness than ever. They had been very disturbed over the turn of events. Although they felt deeply for me, they also had much pity for their father. They told me he had fought the maharaja constantly on this issue. They said there had been many scenes in the palace and that for a long time the Tika Raja had held out. I was surprised to learn from the girls that the Tika Raja's mother had also exerted pressure on her son. The senior maharani had wailed day and night that she wanted to see her grandson before she died and she punctuated each argument with a heart attack; finally the Tika Raja gave in.

It was difficult to understand why the maharani had taken such a stand. All her life she had suffered from the intrusion of other women; one would think that she would have had the compassion not to force it on me, knowing how much she had been hurt by it. Instead, her attitude was that since she had had to put up with plural marriage, why shouldn't I?

I tried to be brave but I was humiliated beyond all measure. There was nothing I could do, however, but pray for the courage to help me through the ordeal. I had to think of my three daughters who were still unmarried. If I had had no such responsibilities I could have left India at once, but I knew that my duty was to see that my girls married well. Until then I had to maintain my position as the Tika Raja's first wife.

The Tika Raja was shamed by his inability to resist his father. Shortly after I arrived in Kapurthala he came to see me. His distress was touching and I could not find it in my heart to be angry with him. I could only feel pity. In many ways he had gotten the worst of it.

Our Western education had made it impossible for us to go backward. The plural marriages which had been accepted by both our parents horrified us. But divorce was out of the question. We had to make the best of our unfortunate situation.

The Tika Raja tried in every way to make my position easier for me. He told me that I need have nothing to do with his second wife and that my home in Kapurthala would always be completely mine. I had full freedom, he said, to come and go as I pleased, and he even presented me with a document which stated that I had the right to do as I wished. It also admitted that, under pressure, he had committed a humiliating wrong against me. Under the Hindu law, this paper offered no legal assurance, but it was a generous gesture on the part of my husband.

The second marriage had been performed quietly without any publicity. But it was not to be expected to remain so. Soon all India rang with the news.

Surprisingly enough, the reaction to the Tika Raja's marriage was unfavorable to the maharaja. It was not I who was publicly humiliated. On every side, blame was heaped on my father-in-law for forcing an unwanted second bride on his heir. For years he had boasted that he was a modern thinker; it was well known that he had insisted on giving the Tika Raja and me a European education. Now it was clear that when it affected him, his talk was only talk.

The fact that I had three daughters proved that I was not unwilling to bear children. It was shameful, said his critics, that because he had no grandson, he had forced his heir to revert to the much-criticized system of plural marriage. Even his fellow rulers, whom the maharaja had decried as "old-fashioned," felt that he had behaved very badly; enlightened Indian society considered themselves betrayed by his actions.

I was touched by the kindnesses which were shown me by many people. Lady Willingdon, who was then vicerine, insisted that I go to Delhi to visit her and the viceroy. This invitation was more than a friendly act; it was a public declaration that the viceroy considered my social position unimpaired by what had happened.

In Delhi people went out of their way to show me how strongly they disapproved of the maharaja's action and from the viceroy's house I was invited to the Maharaja of Kashmir's home with my daughters for the polo season.

It seemed best that I remain in India for the rest of the year. My girls were still upset over the marriage and I wanted to avoid the attack that I was running away from a difficult situation. I knew that for their sake I had to maintain my position as the Tika Rani, at least until they were married.

But the Tika Raja, once again, could not face his own responsibilities. Although he had been married but a few months, early in March he left for Europe leaving behind his new bride. I could not help but feel sorry for her. A simple young Rajput girl from the Kangra Valley, of high birth, without education or experience, she had no resources with which to fight back. She could only dumbly accept what was to be her lot. So, while her husband was in the West, she obediently spent her days with her mother-in-law.

The Tika Raja had placed the family house at Musoorie at my disposal for the summer. At the end of April I took the girls there, while my sister Madhvi and her husband, the Raja of Jasdan, and their tiny girl, Kookoo, rented a house nearby. I was homesick for Europe and longed to see my own friends as I had during my summers abroad for now I needed comfort more than ever. At the same time, it was a delight to be with my daughters. Now they were really growing up and I enjoyed taking them with me to dinners and parties.

There was an unusually heavy monsoon that year and for a time we spent our days in the house as the rain pounded endlessly against the windows. But when the rains were over in September, many old friends arrived in Musoorie and after nine years of summering in Europe it was good to see them again.

In October I took my daughters to Hardwar for a pilgrimage to the holy city. After the torturous winter months I longed to find some peace and hoped that faith, which always seemed just beyond my finger tips, would fill my heart.

I was also bothered by an incident which had occurred in Italy on my last visit. While visiting the Andrea Robillants I had eaten some strangely flavored meat. When I asked what it was, they teasingly told me it was beef. Since beef is the absolutely forbidden food of orthodox Hindus, I turned pale and rushed from the room where I was immediately ill.

When I returned to the table, my friends apologized. It was only a joke, they told me. But I did not know whether to believe them. Their denial might only have come when they saw how disastrously the meal had ended.

I was anxious, therefore, to perform the Hindu rites of purification on the chance that I had unwittingly committed a serious transgression of Hinduism.

I spent my days at Hardwar doing *puja* (repentance) on the banks of the Ganges. With hundreds of others, clad in a cotton sari, I bathed in the icy river. I helped feed the poor and followed each Hindu ritual. I found some comfort in all of this and at the end of our visit felt able to go back to the harsh realities of my life.

In Hardwar I learned that my husband's second wife had just given birth. But he was still doomed to disappointment for the baby was once again a daughter.

I could not help being wickedly amused. At the same time my heart went out to the young bride who had disappointed the maharaja. Hers would not be an easy lot.

I spent a quiet winter in Kapurthala and when spring came around again my daughters and I went back to Musoorie. At that time I decided that I would remain in India for the second year in succession. Since I could not afford to keep my Paris apartment, I disposed of it through my lawyers. It saddened me to give it up for I liked to think that I had a home in Europe, but it was a necessity.

My three girls were growing into charming young women, all self-possessed and good-looking. Indira, the eldest, was the most like me—headstrong and ambitious. Her heart was set on an acting career and it was clear that she would never be content to live conventionally as an Indian princess. The three girls were good friends and I was extremely proud of them.

After another year in India, I decided to return to Europe for a time. My health had been poor again and the doctors advised me to seek consultation in Europe. There was no reason for me to remain any longer in India. I had stayed there long enough to make my position secure. My girls were young ladies now and were busy with their own affairs. I would gladly have taken them to Europe with me but the maharaja flatly refused. Legally, I had no control over my daughters and could not take them from the country without my father-in-law's approval. We all wept when we parted from each other but the girls were worried about my health and were anxious for me to become completely well again.

As for me, I was tired of being an exile in my own country. I was no longer the privileged wife of my husband, nor did I have the status of Westerners who are divorced. I felt as though I had been robbed of everything. In Europe and America no one thought twice about a woman traveling alone or with friends. In India I was an object of pity and contempt.

I had thought much about my life in the past two years I had spent in India. I was well aware that it was now necessary to plan my future. My girls were grown and would soon be married; they did not need me to hover over them. My position in Kapurthala was too untenable. I could not remain there permanently. And yet I was still a fairly young woman; it was too soon for my life to be over.

The peace I had sought in life was not to be found. I was tired of wandering over the earth, yet there was no place that was home. For the moment I found the most comfort from being with my friends. I was lonely. It was better to be sad in the midst of gaiety than to be alone and desperate.

I sailed from Bombay on the Italian liner, *Conte Rosso*, bound for Venice. I visited Milan for some days with the Robillants and then went by train through Switzerland to Germany where I entered a nursing home at Freiburg in Breisgau. There I underwent another operation and remained in bed over six weeks.

It was my first and only visit to Germany. Hitler had already come into power although I saw nothing of Nazism in the nursing home. I had, however, heard enough about the new order and was deeply distressed and worried.

Phillip of Hesse, who was then one of Hitler's leading figures, sent me a basket of carnations and later called me from Kassel. He invited me to his home, saying that he would introduce me to Hitler and Göring. But unfortunately I was too ill to travel then. If I had been able to go I would have had the opportunity perhaps of murdering Hitler. I should have been happy to have given my life to save so many million others.

On my return to Paris I spent the week end at Senlis with the Louis Bromfields. At that time he was talking about a book on India which he believed would be a success. Later his lovely book, *The Rains Came,* surpassed even his expectations.

I visited London and then went on to the Lido in Venice. Always it was the same. Wherever I went there were parties and gaiety but I had lost heart in entertainment. It was something to do but my heart was not so easily mended.

Some time before, on my first visit to America, I had heard about the soybean as a possible way to end starvation in countries such as India. I was amazed to learn at that time of the wonderful potentialities of the bean and of the ease with which enough could be grown to wipe out the plague of hunger across the world. I now had an opportunity to visit America again and it was a chance to find out more about this remarkable product. Perhaps, if I couldn't find happiness in my personal life, at least I could someday help my country.

In New York Mrs. Randolph Hearst gave a dinner and dance in my honor in her home on Riverside Drive and I met again the man who had introduced me to the soybean, Armand Burke, and his Russian colleague, Dr. Horvath. At length we discussed the possibilities of the mass production of the soy products and I left the party fired with enthusiasm for the whole project.

On this visit I decided to go out to the west coast. I wanted to get a better look at America. I was shocked by what I saw in Hollywood.

I had been invited to a house party there but after several days I left and went to a hotel. For two days the guests and the hosts had been drunk and behaved in a fashion I had never seen before in all my travels. But that was only one side of Hollywood and the one I would like to forget.

Later I was entertained by many brilliant and charming people, including Mary Pickford, Charlie Chaplin, Douglas Fairbanks, and Gary Cooper. I visited the studios and went with friends to Malibu Beach, which I found cheerful but disappointing as the sea was too cold for bathing.

I flew back to New York after many hectic weeks in Hollywood. I was there only a short time when I received a cable from my daughter, Indira.

"I have left India without permission," said the wire, "and am on my way to London."

Hurriedly I made preparations to leave and took the first boat to London. I arrived there in time to meet Indira. The moment we were alone she turned to me defiantly.

"I know you're angry," she said, "but I could not bear India another minute."

"You cannot expect me to condone your actions. It was wrong to defy your father and grandfather."

Indira's eyes filled with tears. Her rebellion had slipped away and she looked like a guilty little girl.

"Can't you understand?" she pleaded. "If I had remained, they would have forced me into a marriage of grandfather's choice. I could not stand the thought of such a marriage."

I sighed. I knew in my heart that Indira was right. Even as I had been, she was too rebellious to be forced into a mold. Perhaps this way was best.

"What I don't understand," I asked, "is how did you get the money to come to London?"

Indira looked shamefaced.

"I have been saving my allowance for years," she answered. "I knew that someday I would get to London."

Her determination astonished me. She had been planning this, then, in secret, for a long time. She knew that I would have forbidden the project and also wanted to protect me from any accusation that I had aided her in defying the maharaja.

Now that Indira had made the trip to London there was nothing I could do but try to help her. Walter Pidgeon gave me a letter to Alexander Korda who was kind enough to advise her. However, he tried to discourage her—acting, he said, was a dog's life. But Indira had made up her mind and nothing would change it.

The Royal Academy of Dramatic Art accepted Indira as a student. At once she was absorbed in her work and seemed happier than in many years. In the meantime, the maharaja had stopped her state allowance. I gave her all the money I could but she wanted as little as possible, she said. She wanted to be independent.

I remained in London for two months and in that time I

introduced Indira to many people. They all liked her but Indira made it clear that she wanted to become an actress on her own; she did not want any help from anyone. She was determined to work hard and succeed on merit; I could not help but be proud of her.

It was my first experience of an English winter and I did not enjoy it. As the chill, foggy days drifted by my admiration for the English people grew. It was no wonder that they were able to maintain a stoical character. To survive, it was necessary. As for me, I came down with the flu after only a few weeks.

I was in London the night of January 20, 1936, when the news was flashed that King George V had died. The world as I had known it seemed to be slipping away, not only from death but from the changes that war and progress had made.

After Indira was comfortably settled in rooms of her own, I returned to India. Sushila and Ourmila were wild with curiosity about their sister. At first I pretended to be angry with them for they had been in Indira's confidence for several months before she had run away. But the girls knew that I was proud of Indira's independence and delighted that she was finding happiness in her own way.

"But how does she like European clothes?" they chorused.

I laughed. Indira had never been fond of Western styles. At home she preferred jodhpurs and shorts for everyday and a sari for more formal wear. When I saw her in London she was wearing a European dress she had bought in Bombay, but since Indira had little taste in clothes she was an odd sight. I told the girls that I had scolded her when I saw her but that she had taken it good-humoredly.

"You know I was never much for that sort of thing," she had answered.

Sushila and Ourmila admired Indira for her independence but they had no desire to emulate her. They were more truly Indian girls, quiet, reserved, and without rebellion. Her action in leaving India as she did was inconceivable to them. Neither one of my daughters would have been capable of such independence.

But I thought as I looked at their sweet, smiling faces, eager to hear news of their loved sister, that life would be easier on my younger girls than on Indira. I knew because Indira was her mother's daughter.

Chapter Sixteen

For years Sushila and Ourmila had begged me to take them to Europe, and now that their sister was in London they were all the more anxious to make the trip.

"Please, please, can't we go?" they pleaded.

I looked at their bright faces, so eager for life. Nothing could have given me greater joy than to take my daughters and show them the foreign countries I had learned to love. But there were many obstacles in the way.

"You cannot go," I said firmly, "without the permission of your father and grandfather."

"We know that, Mother," answered Sushila impatiently. "But they will give us permission."

I shook my head doubtfully. I knew the maharaja was still furious with Indira for leaving India. It was not likely that he would allow the girls to go to Europe.

"If you really want to make the trip," I explained, "you

must ask your grandfather. It would do no good if I intervened."

Ourmila and Sushila exchanged mischievous glances. Ourmila giggled.

"Wait and see," she said. "We will come to Europe with you."

I had little hope that the girls would be successful in their venture but I had not counted on their feminine wiles. As I learned later, they had begged and teased, cried and pouted until their grandfather relented. He could not resist such a barrage of femininity, not even from his own granddaughters.

The girls enjoyed every moment of the trip. They were especially grateful that I allowed them to dance in the evenings. They had never had such freedom in India but I felt it was time they left behind some of their restricting old-fashioned rules of conduct.

We stayed in Venice for a week with my old friend, Andy Robillant, and his second wife in their lovely *palazzo*. The girls insisted on seeing everything and we spent a hectic week visiting museums, churches, and gliding on the canals. They had never really traveled before and it was a constant source of amazement to them to discover how different Italy was from India. They had judged the world by their own tiny sphere of life.

It was unfair, declared Andy Robillant, to leave Italy for France without showing the girls more of the country.

"Yes, he is perfectly right," chorused the girls. "At least take us to Rome."

They begged so hard to see the famous city that finally I

gave in and agreed to make the trip to Rome. It was very difficult to get hotel accommodations, for Rome was crowded with visitors. Hitler was expected there on an official state visit to the king.

We finally settled ourselves in a small family hotel where Prince Potranzie, the former governor of Rome and an old friend of mine, had found us rooms. Our days in Rome were just as busy as they had been in Venice—in the mornings the girls and I went sight-seeing; the afternoons and evenings we devoted to social activities.

Hitler was due in Rome on May 3. The Marquise Michiatelli invited us to tea on the occasion at the *Palazzo Buonaparte* which was opposite Mussolini's *Palazzo Venezia*. There was much excitement in Rome that day. Crowds thronged in the streets and it was almost impossible to make your way through the thousands of people milling about. Fortunately, we had been given a police pass or we might never have arrived at the Michiatellis.

There were over a hundred people there when we arrived and in an hour there were more than three hundred. Many of my friends were at the party and it was clear that none of them, particularly the Italians, had any enthusiasm for the German alliance.

At last the procession began in the street below. There were many cheers but not one cheer from the whole crowd for Hitler. They were all for King Victor and the roars of *"Viva il re!"* resounded through the streets.

Later that afternoon we heard that Count Czernin, a close friend of the Duke di Sangro's, had been arrested in the crowd for shouting, "Down with Hitler!" Czernin was an Austrian who had spent many years in Italy. He feared what would happen under an alliance with Hitler.

Once again I saw Prince Phillip of Hesse but it was a cool meeting. We were both polite but he was aware of my views on what was happening in Germany. Phillip had changed with the years. I remembered him as a charming young man. Now he had become an arrogant, self-satisfied member of the Herrenvolk.

I was glad when the party was over and relieved when the Germans left Rome. There was something depressing about their visit—the city seemed gloomy with their presence.

I had promised the girls that they would see Naples so we left Rome by car with several friends and motored by way of Amalfi and Sorrento. By this time I was exhausted from sight-seeing and even Ourmila and Sushila had begun to tire from the trip.

We finally arrived in Paris early in May. Ourmila and I were not well and went at once to bed. She had an acute attack of influenza and I learned that it was necessary for me to have another operation. We made arrangements for the operation to take place the following month.

Indira joined us in Paris and it was a family reunion filled with kisses and happy squeals. The girls exclaimed over their London sister.

"She is a real European now," they said in delight.

The three girls were overjoyed when I sent them back to London together. They gossiped and chattered. It was a lovely sight to see how well they got on with one another. I felt it was best for them to be in London during my operation and convalescence and had arranged with friends there to look after the girls.

In August I was well again and took the girls to Monte Carlo. They were anxious to see the famous gambling resort and I had not been there for a long time. During our stay we motored along the Côte d'Azur and I showed the girls Cannes and the small fishing villages of St. Tropez and St. Raphaël where the red clay cliffs tumble into the bright blue sea.

Meanwhile the Munich crisis developed. All over Europe there was talk of war. For a time in Paris there was real panic. I could not take an optimistic view. For a long time I had been convinced that the Germans meant business. It was not difficult to see that war was inevitable.

I could not decide what to do about the girls. On the one hand, I wanted to keep them away from Kapurthala and its influences as long as possible; on the other hand, the sounds of approaching war terrified me. In the end I talked to many people who were convinced that war would not come that year and I decided to keep them in Europe for at least another ten months.

Paris in the summer of 1939 was gay; it reminded me of 1914. In a sense it was the last desperate attempt to keep away the monster of war which was slowly beginning to strangle the world. The girls enjoyed the gaiety and the parties but I could not relax. Fear gnawed at my heart.

Everywhere they were saying that the Maginot line was impenetrable. Yet there was little optimism in Paris. It was a curious kind of atmosphere. The attitude was that war was inevitable and yet the French refused to believe that it would really happen.

In the beginning of September the blow fell. Hitler attacked Poland and in two days Britain and France declared war on Germany. Still people said war could not last but by now I was really frightened.

Passage was arranged for Ourmila, Sushila, and me on an Italian boat which was leaving for India from Venice. I was worried about Indira and asked the maharaja to help me get her out of England but he refused to lift a finger. In any case, Indira had made up her mind to stay in London. When I finally was able to get a telephone call through the jammed wires, Indira told me that she was driving an ambulance and was determined to remain in England throughout the war. It was her country now, she said with a lump in her throat, and she would not desert it in its time of need. All my arguments to be reasonable were in vain. In the end I had to admire the ideals of my daughter, as well as her bravery.

Back in Kapurthala I found it difficult to settle down. I was worried about Indira although her letters home were cheerful and she seemed to have found a new self-confidence through her war work. Still she was my child and my heart was heavy as I read of the daily bombings which pounded over war-torn London.

We had been home about two months when my sister, Madhvi, wrote to me concerning my daughter, Ourmila. I was surprised to receive her letter but before I made any decision concerning it I consulted Ourmila.

I pointed to the letter tossed on my desk as she sat before me, her bright face questioning.

"The Maharaja of Bhawanagar has invited us to Delhi," I began. "He would like to discuss the possibility of marriage between you and his brother."

Ourmila looked startled.

"Is it necessary that I marry so soon?" she asked in a frightened voice.

I patted her dark hair reassuringly and smiled at her.

"Your happiness is the most important thing in the world to me," I told her. "You need do nothing which will cause you pain."

Ourmila looked at me earnestly.

"I want to do what is right," she said, "and most of all I would like to please you. Do you want me to marry him?"

I thought carefully before answering. Ourmila was a sweet, obedient child who would put my wishes before her own. But I only wanted her happiness.

"My darling," I answered her, "I will leave the decision up to you. But perhaps we should visit Delhi so that you can meet the young man for yourself."

Ourmila, all smiles again, agreed. Some days later we went off in the spirit of adventure to see the Maharaja of Bhawanagar and his brother.

The young man was much taken with Ourmila. I approved of him—he was nice and pleasant-looking—and I liked the way he treated Ourmila. Although I could not say Ourmila was infatuated with him, she seemed to like the young Bhawanagar and when he formally proposed (after obtaining his brother's consent) she accepted and they exchanged engagement rings.

It was decided that the marriage would take place in March. Ourmila and I returned to Kapurthala in order to make preparations for the wedding and soon afterward the Dewan of Bhawanagar arrived to complete the arrangements.

We were discussing the wedding one morning when the door of my study flew open and Ourmila rushed into the room with a telegram in her hand. Her face was pale and she was weeping.

I got out of my chair quickly and ran to Ourmila. My heart was paralyzed with fear when I saw the telegram in her hand. I expected the worst. I could only think of Indira in London. Ourmila threw herself into my arms. She could not speak but thrust the wire into my hands.

"Read it," she sobbed.

I straightened out the telegram which she had crushed in her agitation and read it aloud.

"The Maharaja of Bhawanagar deeply regrets that the match between my brother and Ourmila of Kapurthala must be broken off at once . . ."

The wire went on to say that his wife, the maharani, had gone on a hunger strike in protest against her brother-in-law marrying into the Kapurthala family because the Kapurthalas were Sikhs and not Rajputs. But they had been completely aware of this from the beginning. I was at a loss to understand what had happened.

Later I found out that the maharani had pretended to

agree to the young prince's marriage but she had had no intention of allowing it to be consummated. She and the dewan had plotted to embarrass her husband and his brother. The maharani did not make her protests until after the engagement had been announced publicly. They succeeded. It was humiliating for the maharaja, for the broken engagement received much newspaper publicity.

Ourmila, too, was deeply hurt by it. I wanted to comfort her but it was difficult. Every parent longs to protect his child from the brutality of life and to preserve the happy innocence of babyhood. But there is no way you can prevent life from moving ahead. As Ourmila sobbed in my lap at the treachery and pain she was feeling for the first time, I realized there was little I could do to help her. I had had my own pain and had somehow survived. Somewhere Ourmila would have to find her own courage to help her through the tortures from which no human being is immune.

We could talk to each other, however, and I was grateful for that. Any small measure of comfort I could bring to my daughter was a blessing. I was thankful that my own suffering had taught me compassion for her troubles and not bitterness. In a way, being able to help Ourmila made up a little for the many lonely nights I had wept into my pillow, alone and desolate. There was no way I could change my past but I could try to give my daughter the comfort which I had never had.

I dried Ourmila's tears and wiped her face with cool water.

"Why are you crying, my child?" I asked her gently. "Did you love him so much?"

Ourmila straightened up and looked at me in surprise. "Why, no," she answered candidly. "I didn't love him." She paused a moment and then corrected herself.

"That is, I liked him," she said. And biting her lips in deep thought, she said, "But I cannot say I loved him."

"Then you have nothing to be sad about, have you?" I answered her, taking her cold little hands in mine.

Ourmila stared at me a moment as if she were trying to decide if I were right. Then she burst into tears once more.

"But I am so humiliated," she cried. "Everyone is talking about me. I cannot bear it."

My heart went out to my child. What can you say to relieve the first anguish of the young? Is there a word of comfort to ease the betrayal of the innocent? Ourmila was learning, and in a shocking fashion, that the world is a cold place and that there are those who feed on the misfortunes of others. It would only be through more pain that she would learn there is love and kindness as well.

"My darling Ourmila," I told her, "it will be impossible for you to believe what I am going to tell you now and yet someday you may find that it is so. You should be grateful for this humiliation."

Ourmila's eyes widened in disbelief.

"Grateful?" she exclaimed. "How can you say such a thing? Do you mean because I did not love him?"

"That is part of it," I answered. "It would have been wrong for you to marry a man you do not love. But that has nothing to do with the humiliation. I said that because it is better if you can learn how little pride has to do with happiness. I have suffered much humiliation in my life. Yet it has taught me that strength is to be found in other places. Pride is a crumbling rock on which to lean."

Ourmila did not answer but she seemed soothed by my words. And in the weeks which passed she bravely tried to have courage. She was no longer my baby. The experience had changed her into a woman.

During the summer we spent our time in Simla in a house loaned to us by the Maharaja of Patiala. By some curious twist of fate, the house was but a stone's throw from the home of our cousins, the Raja and Rani of Jubbal. Although we had reconciled after my father's death, I had not seen them since. I was aware that the raja still bitterly resented my marriage into the Kapurthala family and I made no overtures to them for that reason.

But when the raja's daughter, Illa, was to be married, my sister Kamla, who was staying with me in Simla, received an invitation to the wedding. Shortly afterward, Kamla brought the young bride to see me. After the wedding I decided to call on my Jubbal cousins and an invitation to tea followed. The raja and his rani received us graciously and soon afterwards the Jubbal boys began coming to our house and quickly made friends with Ourmila and Sushila. Some weeks later I gave an afternoon party for about fifty of the young people and the Raja of Jubbal came with his sons.

It was during that summer that France capitulated. At the time I had been trying to raise funds for a motor ambulance to be sent to the French government and we had collected a sizeable amount of money when the news came. My poor little French maid was prostrated and refused to eat or speak for days. My heart went out to all my friends who were living in the terror of that dreadful defeat.

My sister Kamla, who had refused many offers of marriage because she would not enter an orthodox Hindu household, became engaged shortly after we returned to Kapurthala. Her husband-to-be was making an excellent career for himself in the Indian army and she was radiant with happiness. The marriage took place in New Delhi in November and I gave a large reception at the Imperial Hotel for both Indian and European guests. I was touched at the unexpected arrival of young Birendra Singh, the fourth son of the Raja of Jubbal, who came, he said, to pay respect to Kamla's marriage.

Shortly after the wedding I learned that a young maharaja wanted to discuss the possibility of an engagement to Ourmila. Remembering the Bhawanagars, I proceeded very cautiously but finally decided to discuss the whole idea with Ourmila.

Ourmila blushed profusely when I told her the news. She bent her head shyly for a moment, then lifted her chin and gazed at me solemnly.

"I could not marry him," she said earnestly. "You see, I have promised to marry Birendra Singh of Jubbal."

I was aghast at this news. I knew only too well what my Jubbal cousins thought about the Kapurthala family. But Ourmila would not listen to argument.

"We will wait," she said bravely, "until the Raja of Jubbal gives his consent. If he refuses completely, then we will have to marry without it."

In spite of the difficulties which lay ahead for Ourmila I was glad for her. It was easy to see that this was a love match. Only good could come of such strong feeling.

When Birendra Singh arrived in Kapurthala I had a long talk with him. He was both straightforward and ardent. He told me that he had not approached his parents on his marriage and I persuaded him to wait a year before doing so. Ourmila and he would be allowed to correspond freely and to see each other whenever possible. Then if they still felt the same after twelve months, he was to seek his parents' permission to marry her. Birendra Singh told me that he was deeply in love with Ourmila and that the separation was a cruelty but he promised to do as I wished.

It was at this time that I had a partial reconciliation with my father-in-law. I had heard rumors that he desired such a reconciliation and I had already forgiven him the pain he had caused me in my life. Many times I had had bitter thoughts toward him but in the end I realized that he could not help himself. He was not equipped to have lived otherwise and in his own way he had done his best.

One afternoon as I was walking in my garden the maharaja's car drew up. He got out and walked slowly toward me. I had not seen him for several years and I was shocked at the change in his appearance. His vigor and self-assurance were gone and he was an aged, tired man. I could not help but pity him.

Yet his greeting was characteristic of our whole relationship.

No sooner had we exchanged a few pleasantries when he

said, "I must congratulate you on marrying off your brothers and sisters so well. I hope you can do the same for Sushila and Ourmila; otherwise they will follow the example of Indira."

For a moment my temper flared as it had in the old days but I was able to control myself now. I tried to answer calmly.

"You must know," I said, "that the girls are free to marry men of their own choice. Otherwise it would be better for them not to marry at all."

"Hmmph," said maharaja but he did not press the point. He, too, was tired of war and was ready for a reconciliation with me at last.

At the end of June, Ourmila's fiancé came up on a ten-day leave. Now that he was in the army and about to go on active service he was determined to marry Ourmila at once. He admitted that he had begged his parents' permission but although his mother was willing, my cousin, the Raja of Jubbal, absolutely refused to hear of it. Birendra Singh had made up his mind to marry Ourmila in spite of his father's refusal and since Ourmila pleaded with me, too, I felt I could not stand in their way. So I gave my consent to an immediate wedding.

There were only four days at our disposal; I had no time to invite anyone formally. My husband and father-in-law wired their consent to the marriage from Kashmir but would not be able to arrive in time for the ceremony. In the breathless hum of activity, I invited over a hundred people verbally and the wedding turned out to be a successful and joyful occasion.

The next day Ourmila and Birendra Singh left for Bombay where he had to rejoin his regiment. Just before we parted, Ourmila came into my room. She was beautiful with the happiness of a bride. She threw her arms around me and kissed me. She was crying and laughing at the same time.

"You've been so good to me, Mother," she said. "How can I ever thank you for giving me this happiness?"

There was no answer to make to my child. I had already had my reward. It was enough to see her happy in a way I had never known.

Chapter Seventeen

As I look back now on the days of the second world war, they seemed to fly by, but at the time it was not so. For us, as everywhere else outside of India, they were harassing years, filled with apprehension.

But even from such times come some good memories. Early in the war my daughter Sushila fell in love with the brother of the Maharaja of Bharatpur. Girraj Saran Singh was a bright young officer in the Royal Indian Air Force. When he proposed to Sushila I felt that he was too young for immediate marriage but he declared if he were not allowed to marry Sushila at once he would go up in his airplane and never come down again! Shushu seemed in love and happy at the thought of marriage to her young man and I could not deny them my consent. However, I stipulated that the matter would have to be discussed with the Maharaja of Bharatpur before it was settled.

I met the maharaja in Delhi. We agreed that the marriage would take place but we completely disagreed on one point. The maharaja wanted my assurance that Sushila would consent to remain in purdah whenever she was in the state of Bharatpur.

"How can you even suggest such a thing?" I asked.

The maharaja shrugged his shoulders.

"I'm afraid that must be part of our agreement," he answered.

"Then Sushila may not marry your brother," I answered sharply. "For I would never give my consent to such an outdated and outrageous idea. All my life I have fought against purdah!"

I was genuinely shocked at his demands. It was bad enough that I had had to endure some of the stigma of Indian womanhood—I could not possibly condone it for my daughter. I was also surprised at the maharaja. He had spent twelve years in England during his education—surely this was not the result?

In the end, the Maharaja of Bharatpur gave in and I conceded that on state occasions Shushu would not drive in an open car or carriage through the streets of Bharatpur.

Through all the negotiations Sushila floated in a state of joyfulness. She was not interested in our discussions of her marriage; she had only eyes for her young husband-to-be. The wedding took place in Kapurthala several months later; because of the war it was a simple, quiet ceremony.

About a year later a son, Arnep Singh, was born to Sushila and in 1944 Ourmila gave birth to a daughter. It was hard to believe that I was a grandmother already but it was a delight beyond anything I had yet experienced. In a sense I enjoyed being with my children's babies more than I had when the girls were small. Perhaps the removal of one generation makes for more understanding. When I was bearing children I was so absorbed in my own problems that I was not always able to enjoy their care. Now it was different. In a way my life was solved. I could get pleasure from simpler pursuits.

I spent much of my time in war work and in the political problems of India. There was so much to be done. I was still actively trying to develop the soybean. It seemed to me that a starving nation could not begin to think until its stomach was full. But it was difficult to do it by myself. Everywhere I went I found indifference and even obstacles put in my way.

The more I learned about my country, the more shocked I became. I realized that there are more than sixty million untouchables—almost half of the population of the United States. These people cannot work in any but the most menial jobs and are not allowed to come into contact in any way with the rest of the vast population of India. Most of them are starving and their little children lie on the hot, dusty streets of India with their stomachs bulging from malnutrition and their eyes cloudy with hopelessness.

And yet, as a woman, it seemed I could do little. Even the men who had accomplished so much for my country were often helpless before the enormity of the problem. I was particularly awed by the work of Nehru and admired the leadership he had shown in our country.

I met Pandit Nehru the first time at a dinner given at

the Nepal Consulate. He was a striking-looking man with a moody face and a temperamental manner. But from the first word his brilliance was immediately evident.

He was not interested in social conversation and we discussed the problems of educating masses of illiterate people who were wary of knowledge, as if it were an evil spirit. I agreed with his ideas completely and yet it was hard to see how they could be accomplished—at least in our lifetimes.

"The independence of India is a good thing," I said to Nehru. "But in order for it to work, India will need fifty thousand Nehrus to rule it."

I met Nehru for the second time at a large garden party where hundreds of Indians and Europeans were gathered. He did not smile at all that day but seemed to be irritated. He looked so angry I was nearly afraid to greet him but I had enjoyed our first talk so much I finally got up the courage to walk over to him.

"I despise these parties," he told me and he seemed so angry that his hands could scarcely hold the teacup.

"It *is* crowded," I answered innocently.

He put down his cup and turned to me, nearly glaring.

"It's not that," he answered. "What I can't understand is how people can have these parties when the world is in upheaval."

I could not resist teasing this stern man.

"Then why do you come here?" I asked him demurely.

For a moment Nehru looked severe. Then his eyes twinkled and he smiled at me. After that I had the courage to tell him a few words about my soybean project.

Mr. Nehru listened to me and then said, "I cannot attend to everything. Go and see my Food Minister."

"But he will never believe me," I said.

"Use my name and tell him I asked you to see him," Mr. Nehru said kindly.

I did see him and found Mr. Munshi sympathetic to my plan.

It was a great occasion meeting Mahatma Gandhi, a man for whom I had always had the most enormous amount of admiration. I could not agree with him on everything for it seemed to me that he overlooked the fact that it is not easy for man to become perfect. The Mahatma's own struggle for perfection was so much fulfilled that few others have the will or ability to become as saintly as he.

Once I questioned him about the unrest of the people.

"Perhaps it would have been kinder," I said, "to have begun with the education of the upper class. The poor have become discontented but they do not seem to be better off. Would not the other way have been better?"

Gandhi frowned a moment before answering.

"Reform cannot come from the upper class," he said. "They have nothing to gain by it. It must come from the people who are downtrodden."

I realized the truth in what he said. And yet I wondered how long it would take to change a country as backward as India. Out of four hundred million people there are not three million who are really educated.

After the war was over I returned to Europe. I was shocked by the changes I found there. Europe seemed defeated and broken in a way I had never dreamed possible. The war had taken a toll in the spirit of the people. Everywhere was confusion. I could see that a new era was beginning and that the world I had known was fast disappearing. No one could say for sure which way of life was better. Times of transition always bring turmoil, and Europe seemed completely disrupted after its toil of war.

In India everything was changed as well. When I went back to Kapurthala after two years in Europe and America, I found the state nearly in ruins. The terrible famine after the war had brought devastation and disease to my country. I wept when I saw my little home in Kapurthala. My small garden was gone, dried up and run over with weeds. The house was dilapidated and the servants had fled to Pakistan. The surrounding villages were empty and desolate—it was almost as though an earthquake had destroyed the country.

My father-in-law seemed old and sick. I wanted to discuss the dreadful conditions in Kapurthala but he was too ill to be rational. The maharaja was living in the past; he could only speak of the good days.

As I looked at his exhausted, lined face, I could see the pallor of death beginning to creep over his features. He babbled incessantly about returning to Europe and America and made plans for the years ahead as if he expected to live forever. I could not help but feel sorry for him. He was suffering agonies but his pride would not let him admit it.

I left Kapurthala for Bharatpur where I stayed two months. I returned home in order to see my father-in-law who had written me to come and see him before he went to Europe. I was dismayed that he was planning to make such a trip. He looked more aged than in the months past and I advised him to remain at home with his nurses and doctors. But he was determined to go.

It was necessary for him to have an operation and he wanted to have the surgery done in France. He planned to leave Kapurthala for Bombay in March and sail from there to Europe. He seemed worried this time about his health but his fear drove him to exert himself as if not giving in would save his life. It was a dreadful sight to see the shaking old man of seventy-seven pull himself out of bed and try to walk to his chair. During my visit he had all his famous white teeth pulled and although he was brave I could see what an emotional shock it had been.

When I said good-by to him, I bent down and kissed his cheek for the first time in many years. I suddenly had the feeling that I would never see him again and in spite of the differences we had had through the years, I had known the maharaja all my life. I did not respect him but he was part of my world and despite all his faults and mistakes he always was a sincere champion of India. He had done much abroad to create goodwill toward our country.

I was in Cooch-Behar when my father-in-law made his trip to Bombay. I planned to stay in Cooch-Behar until June and was trying to arrange a trip to America via Honolulu when I received a telegram from Bombay. My father-in-law had died there.

My daughter called me from Simla and told me to go immediately to Kapurthala as the cremation would take place there. I tried to book passage on a plane but because of the heavy monsoon, all planes were grounded. The best I could do was to travel by train. It was a long, slow journey and before we reached Calcutta we had to change three times. In Calcutta I received a wire from my husband that his father's body had been flown on a special chartered plane from Bombay and that by the time I reached Kapurthala the ceremonies would be over. On that account, he advised me to change my plans and join my daughter in Simla.

I canceled all the arrangements I had made for my trip to America. My position would now be that of maharani. It would be necessary for me to remain in India to help my husband settle certain affairs of family.

When I returned to Kapurthala I saw my husband and we discussed his father for a long time. The late maharaja had not been a wise ruler, yet there had been much against him from the start. At the age of five his parents had died and he became the ruling power in the hands of unscrupulous guardians. His education had been haphazard and his moral upbringing completely neglected. Was it little wonder that he had turned from his duties as monarch to the pursuit of pleasure in the capitals of Europe?

I remember conversations I had had with the maharaja on the subject, when I urged him to look around him and see the havoc which was being wrought by his incompetent ministers.

"*L'état, c'est moi!*" he would say. "*Après moi le déluge.*"

I could not help showing my anger at this.

"Are you content for your son to be a second *Louis Seize?*" I retorted.

But the maharaja only shook his head and laughed heartily. When he was not angry at my seriousness, he was amused by it.

But now his reign was over and with it a new day had

come for India. Now that she had gained her independence another era was beginning. I wondered how my husband would fare in his lifetime.

As for me, I was still a wanderer. I was no longer of the East nor was I able to accept completely the tempo of a Western culture into which I had not been born. In a sense, the pleasure of traveling had slipped away even as my youth had gone. Now I saw that in some way every place was the same, that the problems of living were similar for people of all lands, and that wherever you went, whether it was a magic island set in the blue crystal sea of the Mediterranean or in the middle of the desert with the hot sands howling about, getting through each twenty-four hours of a day was the most a human being could expect from life.

Once again I turned to my religion for comfort. The spirit of the Gita had somehow eluded me throughout my lifetime yet this time there was no conflict. I did not have to relinquish the world; it had already happened without any effort on my part. I began to see that there is no way you can give up desire. If you are patient, desire will give you up.

As I read, I wondered if I had ever known love. Love, says the Gita, knows no bargaining. Wherever there is any seeking for something in return, there can be no real love; it becomes a mere matter of shopkeeping. Nor does love know fear, for true love casts out all terror.

Such love between men and women seems almost an impossibility. Perhaps the closest I came to it was with my children. With them I was able to love, expecting nothing in return. I did not even want them to look back in my direction; I only wanted them to go forward to find their own happiness.

Some months after the death of my father-in-law I made a trip to London to see my daughter Indira. Sushila and Ourmila were settled and happy now. They had children and seemed satisfied and contented with the way their lives had gone.

But Indira had always worried me. As much as I wanted her happiness I was always nagged by the thought that she would not find it easily. She was too much like me.

I went at once to her tiny apartment in London. It was bleak and rather cheerless in the fashion of many English flats and Indira seemed quieter and, I thought, sadder than when I had last seen her.

But she protested when I remarked on it.

"No, Mother," she said quickly. "I am quite well and happy. You must not worry about me."

But a mother's intuition cannot be so easily dismissed.

"Indira," I asked her, "I know that something is wrong. Perhaps I can help you. Won't you tell me?"

Indira walked to the other end of the room, where she stood near a window. She did not look at me.

"You can't know what it has been like," she said. "It has been so difficult."

"Life is not easy for anyone," I answered.

Indira shook her head. "That's not so," she retorted. "My own sisters, Sushila and Ourmila, are not so tormented as I."

"You cannot make yourself be what you are not. You did not want a conventional family life. You wanted to be an actress."

"Yes," answered Indira. "I wanted to be an actress. But I am not an actress. The theater is so difficult. I have not had the success I wanted. All I have is a stupid little job with a photographer."

"Dearest Indira," I said as gently as I could. "Life holds no guarantee. You did the best you could. And if you failed it was not because you did not try. It was only because things sometimes work out that way."

"I guess you are right," she said slowly. "I was not content to remain in India and marry like my sisters. I would never have been happy that way."

"You see, my child," I told her, "we must all fulfill our own destinies. You could not fight your ambition and intelligence. You had to break away and rebel in your own way."

Indira nodded.

"You must never regret it," I added. "All you can do is go and try to find happiness where it lies for you. Do not envy others. Their solution would give you nothing."

"Your life has not been an easy one," said Indira in sudden compassion. "How did you stand it?"

I thought for a moment. I did not know myself how I had been able to come through certain devastating experiences. And yet the courage to live had come from somewhere, probably from my atavism—centuries of Hindu patience, forbearance, and equanimity.

"Even now," I said, "although I am older and more settled, life is never static. There is always some problem to be faced from day to day."

Indira stood up and pressed her hands to her forehead. "But why is it that nothing seems to be going right for me?"

I caught Indira by the arm and turned her so that she faced me.

"You see," I said, "that is exactly what I mean. And you must not blame yourself. For that is what life is like. You must go on, knowing that there will always be something."

I kissed Indira tenderly good-by. But in my heart I knew she would not change. Her life would be filled with the same rebellion and expectations I had known. I knew that her sisters did have an easier lot because of their simple natures.

But I also knew that there was no other way for Indira. She would have to find herself. My sighs were for the suffering which lay ahead. But I believed that someday she, too, even as I, would find the peace that goes beyond pain.

AUTHORS GUILD BACKINPRINT.COM EDITIONS are fiction and nonfiction works that were originally brought to the reading public by established United States publishers but have fallen out of print. The economics of traditional publishing methods force tens of thousands of works out of print each year, eventually claiming many, if not most, award-winning and one-time best-selling titles. With improvements in print-on-demand technology, authors and their estates, in cooperation with the Authors Guild, are making some of these works available again to readers in quality paperback editions. Authors Guild Backinprint.com Editions may be found at nearly all online bookstores and are also available from traditional booksellers. For further information or to purchase any Backinprint.com title please visit www.backinprint.com.

Except as noted on their copyright pages, Authors Guild Backinprint.com Editions are presented in their original form. Some authors have chosen to revise or update their works with new information. The Authors Guild is not the editor or publisher of these works and is not responsible for any of the content of these editions.

THE AUTHORS GUILD is the nation's largest society of published book authors. Since 1912 it has been the leading writers' advocate for fair compensation, effective copyright protection, and free expression. Further information is available at www.authorsguild.org.

Please direct inquiries about the Authors Guild and Backinprint.com Editions to the Authors Guild offices in New York City, or e-mail staff@backinprint.com.